The quarterly publication of quotable writers

Double Issue
Eighteen: Accommodation
Nineteen: Trial & Error
Spring, 2016

The Quotable

The quarterly publication of quotable writers

www.thequotablelit.com
facebook.com/thequotable
twitter.com/thequotablelit

EDITORS/FOUNDERS
Eimile Campbell, Fiction/Nonfiction
Lisa Heins Vincent, Fiction/Nonfiction
Leslye PJ Reaves, Managing Editor

GUEST EDITOR
Kelly Avery

POETRY EDITOR
Shannon Curtin

COPY EDITOR
Breanne Seidle

Copyright © 2016 by The Quotable, LLC. All rights reserved.
The Quotable is published quarterly by The Quotable, LLC.
No portion of this publication may be reprinted in any form, printed or electronic, without written permission from the creators. All rights to the works printed herein remain with their respective authors or creators.

ISBN: 978-1530782161

Table of Contents

Café	8
T.E. Cowell	8
Dress	10
Julie R. Enszer	10
Tolerance	12
Julie R. Enszer	12
A Home for Kayla	14
Kevin Finnerty	14
After Waking	23
Ann Hillesland	23
Anna Maria Has a Name Like Hills	25
Elaine Kehoe	25
Visions	34
G. Evelyn Lampart	34
Moonlight Knocking	38
Mia-Francesca Mcauslan	38

Forgotten Coast River Ark	40
Karla Linn Merrifield	40
Second Thoughts	41
Lynsey Morandin	41
Riverside Living	46
Roisín O'Donnell	46
That Scene in "Jaws"	48
Joseph Nieves	48
Appetite	50
Keli Osborn	50
Trappings	52
Melissa Ostrom	52
After-Images	54
Alyse Richmond	54
Numerical Happenstance	55
Ruth Sabath-Rosenthal	55
Clean Dogs	57
Matthew Walsh	57
Pink	65

Scott Wordsman	65
I stare down ash	69
E. Kristin Anderson	69
Birds on a Wire	71
E. Kristin Anderson	71
We haven't forgotten about you, motherfucker	72
E. Kristin Anderson	72
Sometimes Writing's Like That	73
Jane Attanucci	73
Albino	74
Eliza Callard	74
Witch Holes	75
Mary Crosbie	75
Full Transparency	80
John Domenichini	80
Rose Salt	84
Embe Charpentier	84
Not Quite Right	88
Michael Gray	88

Week in Life of Professor	97
Drew Guerra	97
purusha.	101
Samantha Guss	101
the funeral pyre.	103
Samantha Guss	103
according to the door frame next to the refrigerator	105
Kate LaDew	105
The Fog	106
Jillian Grant Lavoie	106
Perpetual Motion	113
Jared Levy	113
Error-Prone	117
Robert Manaster	117
Torn House	119
Garrett Rowlan	119
Lines	124
Rebecca Thill	124

Accommodation

"Life is a journey that must be traveled no matter how bad the roads and accommodations."

— Oliver Goldsmith

FICTION

Café
T.E. Cowell

Apart from our age and sex, we had some similarities. We sat in the same café, for instance, drinking coffee from the same size cups. We'd look up every now and then from our respective reading material to notice people, cars passing on the street, the changing morning light coming in through the windows. What we read was different, but the fact that we were both always reading was a similarity. You read books of different lengths. One looked about as big as a dictionary. I was impressed by your stamina, by your apparent thirst for knowledge. One time when you closed the big book and got up for a coffee refill, I casually walked over to your table and glanced at the spine. It was *Ulysses*. You were reading *Ulysses* in a café—something about this struck me as wonderful. I took you very seriously after that, and because of your age, assumed you were in college. I assumed you wanted to be a writer, too, due to all the books you read, and assuming you wanted to be a writer I both admired and felt a little sorry for you. I wished you luck with all your future endeavors, and though I hardly doubted you, I thought you'd be better off studying something more practical. Engineering, for instance. Something you could make a comfortable living doing. If you were my daughter, I thought...

We never said a word, not to each other. We never needed to, it seemed. I arrived at the café about twenty minutes earlier than you did each morning, and when you arrived we'd glance at each other, smile, and sometimes nod politely, and that would seem like enough, like more than enough. I like to think that we felt and appreciated each other's presence more acutely because of our silence. Our silence seemed to speak an agreeable, subtle language.

Then one morning you didn't show up at the café, and in consequence I found it a challenge just getting through the paper. I missed your presence terribly. A week went by and I didn't see you once. I got it in my head that you'd moved somewhere else. If you were indeed taking college courses, I wondered if maybe you'd graduated, or if you'd transferred to a different college. I wondered if maybe one of your parents was sick, or if you'd been offered a job in another town. I wondered lots of things, and finally I stopped wondering. You were gone, and for whatever the reasons, nothing would change the fact.

 I continued to miss your silent presence. Then I started frequenting another café, because I didn't like looking at your empty table. The new café isn't the same, of course, not without you here. I read the paper just as before, just as I've always done since retiring and not having a job to go to. I read the paper and drink my coffee and look up every now and then at people and cars passing on the street and the changing morning light that comes in through the windows. I do all this like I'd done in the previous café, yet something fundamental seems to be missing now from the quality of my mornings, and I know that it is you.

T. E. Cowell lives on an island in Washington State. To view more of his fiction, go here: tecowell4.wordpress.com.

POETRY

Dress
Julie R. Enszer

> It is not the dress we want, but the life we will live in that dress
> —Diana Vreeland

I confess, I am buying
Eileen Fisher dresses
on eBay without abandon.
Black. Blue. Brown. Charcoal grey.
I wear them with brightly-colored
tights. They are long, drape
below my knees, one nearly
to my ankles. I wear them
with scarves and boots,
brown leather boots and
bulky wool sweaters, my hair
tied back in a bun, a few
wisps around my neck.

It is not the dresses I want,
though I need them to teach;
I want the life I imagine
living in these dresses.
A life I imagined when
I began college, when we walked
at dusk the tree-lined streets

of Ann Arbor after milkshakes,
looking at the large houses
of professors, when we read
poems aloud late into the night,
when I saw in your eyes
for the first time what it was
to be loved. I need these dresses;
I want that life.

Tolerance
Julie R. Enszer

We have beautiful photographs
from our wedding;
small intimate ones—
our banded fingers,
looking into each others eyes
just before the ceremony,
cupcakes and flowers—
and large celebratory ones—
the New York Skyline,
a panorama of guests
witnessing our vows—
but the one I return to,
the one we never had developed,
is of my mother
alone on a low chair
she looks slightly ill
she looks like she is about to cry.

This is the mother I remember
She hated that I am a lesbian
but loved how tolerant she became.

In her last years, she said,
See, Julie, I can tolerate
these perversions

I still give you money
I give you presents
it is not so bad.

Some days, I look at that photograph
and whisper
I didn't kill you
as you said I would
and even though you wished
me dead
you didn't kill me either.

When I feel bold, confident,
I whisper to my dead mother:
She still loves me.
Kim, my Kim still loves me.

Everything you told me
was not true.

Julie R. Enszer, PhD, is a scholar and a poet. She is the author of *Sisterhood* (Sibling Rivalry Press, 2013) and *Handmade Love* (A Midsummer Night's Press, 2010). She is editor of *Milk & Honey: A Celebration of Jewish Lesbian Poetry* (A Midsummer Night's Press, 2011). *Milk & Honey* was a finalist for the Lambda Literary Award in Lesbian Poetry. She has her MFA and PhD from the University of Maryland. She is the editor of *Sinister Wisdom*, a multicultural lesbian literary and art journal, and a regular book reviewer for the *Lambda Book Report* and *Calyx*. You can read more of her work at www.JulieREnszer.com.

FICTION

A Home for Kayla

Kevin Finnerty

I've represented fourteen-year-old Kayla Harrison for almost three years. Most of the time she looks as if she's seventeen but acts like she's eleven. Sometimes, it's reversed. I'm not sure what to make of her today. She enters my office wearing a T-shirt depicting a female mouse bent over a toilet purging and immediately sits with her feet up on the seat with her arms wrapped around her knees.

I'd tell her that's not a proper way for a young lady to sit, but there are more important behaviors to address. Anyway, it's not my chair.

I work in the law school's legal clinic as one of two staff attorneys focused on family law. Our space lacks the elegance of the classrooms where the faculty lecture students on corporate, patent and other areas of the law, but it's a step above the downtown legal clinic with its random collection of donated furniture where I used to work.

Today's the first time I've seen Kayla since I returned from maternity leave two weeks ago. And the first time since we sent Kayla to live in a foster home.

I wish I had a law student with me to ease the transition, but the one who previously worked on Kayla's case recently graduated, and the school curtailed the number of summer interns it hired during my absence. So I'm alone with the teenager.

We meet in advance of tomorrow's emergency hearing. The Court needs to assign Kayla to new housing. Kayla stares at me as if I should propose a solution, but I only suggest she wear different clothes tomorrow.

"I didn't do anything wrong," she tells me.

That depends, I find myself thinking like a lawyer. Everything depends on other things in our analysis. In Kayla's case, it depends on how one defines *wrong.* And the ability of a fourteen-year-old girl to consent to sexual activity. And the ability of a fifteen-year-old boy to do the same. As well as the ability of two young teenagers who are thrown together but not blood-related to consider themselves members of the same family unit and not as objects of sexual desire and experimentation.

I tell the kid she's right because she's more right than not right.

Her father, Ryan, abused her. Verbally and physically. Her mother, Dyann, all too often failed to correct behavior in need of correction, and the Court, upon my recommendation, sent her to a foster home, where she met and began having intercourse with her foster brother.

So what are we to do now?

"Just let me go home."

Kayla sees my dubious glance when I lift my eyes from her file, which had been acting more as a shield than a source of information.

I've known the Harrison family, or at least about them, for longer than I care to remember. Ryan and Dyann make for an odd couple. They frequently fight in public but almost universally rally when any outsider calls into question a family practice. At times, they do good work, not just for themselves but the community at large. But Ryan increasingly engages in erratic behavior. It's as if he's concluded the only way to prove he's a worthy family man is by destroying everything he claims makes his family special.

I want to engage Kayla. I hope we can reach a consensus before tomorrow's hearing. The judge will make up his own mind, but if a teenager and her guardian ad litem are unified, it carries a lot of weight. But I can't decide on a course of action myself, so I don't rush to persuade Kayla.

"I'll run away, I swear to God, I will," she tells me when I broach the subject of another short-term foster care.

"I'd never let the court place you in that kind of environment again."

"You did before. And then walked away."

"You know that's not true. I was on leave."

I feel bad about using the birth of my own child as an excuse and implicitly shifting blame to my colleague, who had more than enough on his plate without having to monitor my cases as well. But I have to re-connect with Kayla. I need to make her believe she can trust someone, even if it's the person who thought little about her during her six months on leave and failed to learn what had occurred until her return.

"I thought you were on my side."

"I'm absolutely on your side."

"Then help me."

"How?"

"By doing what I want."

"You know that's not how it works."

How it's supposed to work is each of the parents, or the parents jointly if they wish, has an advocate arguing on his or her behalf. The guardian ad litem acts in the best interests of the child, which is not always (not frequently, in fact) the same as what the child wants. Finally, the child can speak on her own behalf. When the individual involved is as old as Kayla, the Court generally gives the child's expressed desire more weight. But ultimately the judge decides what to do.

I've practiced family law for almost ten years now and while being the guardian ad litem used to be my favorite role, I now find myself longing for the times when I just represent a mother or father, warts and all, and argue on their behalf to the best of my ability. Maybe I don't feel any better about what I do in those cases, but the work is easier.

"Will they send me right from court?"

Kayla finally lets her feet fall to the floor. Her legs begin to bounce. And tremble.

"I don't know."

She sighs and curls away from me, obviously not believing me, though I gave her an honest answer. I don't know what will happen in this case.

The family courtroom looks and feels different than the rest of the courthouse. Cushions and curtains cover the wood and marble found elsewhere, and once a week one finds a teddy bear or doggie left on a table or in a pew.

Most of those Kayla's age who come here bring an attitude. They almost universally carry experiences with drugs and sex. They often appear before the Court as the victims, and occasionally the perpetrators, of crimes of violence.

Kayla walks in wearing a plain white T-shirt and pink shorts, each at least one size too small. I know she's tried to heed my advice, and the items probably were appropriate enough when she was twelve, but I now imagine them enticing fifteen or sixteen-year-old boys into believing she wishes to encourage amorous behavior.

She sits in the first pew. I ask her to join me at the table. She does so meekly.

Judge Clemons enters the room looking like someone who has just presided over a vicious custody hearing, which I know to be the case. I'm sure his brain still functions, but his soul could use a respite.

Judge Clemons offers everyone a half-smile in recognition of familiar faces counter-balanced with the disappointment concerning the circumstances leading to the reunion. He briefly sucks on the bottom half of his bushy, white mustache.

"Counsel, counsel," he says, nodding to my counterpart and then to me.

I almost laugh at the formality. We're not a by-the-book, let's-put-all-this-on-the-record sort of jurisdiction. Especially not in family court. Were our clients not present, I'm sure Judge Clemons would have addressed the lawyers by our first names.

He knows all the family law practitioners in the area. Knows us so well, he invariably grasps when we truly believe the position we take as human beings and when we argue the way we do because we're legal advocates assigned a particular role in the system. Most of all, Judge Clemons understands when there isn't a good solution to a problem.

"Shall we begin?"

It's a rhetorical. We all know we're knee-deep into the shit already.

Q. Daniel Simms, my least favorite, semi-frequent adversary, stands and leans forward confidently. It's not that he's a terrible person or that he's unethical. It's just so over-the-top with him.

"It's an outrage that this Court continues to keep my clients and their daughter apart, given the sort of parenting that takes place in this country. The Harrisons are the sort of family to which others aspire. The actions designed to undermine their autonomy are the product of a few individuals who wish to threaten their way of life."

Judge Clemons and I share a knowing glance. I know that he knows this sort of blather isn't helpful. Q.D., as I call him, always says these sorts of things no matter the circumstances or client.

Q.D. handles divorces between souses of significant wealth much more often than what I consider true family court cases, but the Harrisons have money to burn and they choose to burn some on Q.D., so he puts on a show.

I find the union strange. Q.D. wears custom-tailored suits; he studies and follows fashion trends. But he's overweight and nonathletic, and most people find him socially inept outside a courtroom.

Ryan always wears a black T-shirt and worn jeans despite his blessed bank accounts. They highlight the muscular physique of the former athlete. Men and women gravitate towards Ryan whenever he enters a room. Only some come to realize that he uses his appearance, like his wealth, to take advantage of those susceptible to the superficial.

Ryan gets to his feet before Q.D. has finished and starts speaking over his own counsel. I turn my body away from him, partly so I don't have to look, partly to shield Kayla.

"This whole proceeding is ridiculous."

"Your Honor, I apologize for my client."

"No need to apologize, Dan," Ryan says. "I know you're trying to help, but I refuse to accept that this Court has a right to intrude in this family matter any longer."

"You do?" Judge Clemons opens his eyes wide. I'm not sure if that's a sign of suspicion or growing alertness now that someone has interrupted Q.D.'s canned speech.

Q.D. takes a seat and throws his flabby arms across a couple of chairs.

"What happens to a family in the home is no business of the government."

"Whose business is it?"

"That's between the father, mother, child and God. So it's fair to conclude that the actions of this Court over these last few years have infringed upon my religion."

"Your religion requires that you abuse your daughter?"

"You believe this guy?" Ryan says as he turns around and addresses the non-existent audience in the back of the courtroom. He jerks his thumb towards Judge Clemons. "I've never abused anyone. I've protected my daughter as best I know how. I don't apologize for any acts I've taken in this regard. My only regret is having failed to protect my son the same way."

"Please excuse my husband."

Dyann gets to her feet. She's more frail and sports more gray hair than her husband. One might initially mistake her for Ryan's mother rather than his wife.

Kayla's file suggests Dyann once had a drinking problem, but her mind is sharper and more focused than Ryan's. I once held hope for Kayla with Dyann. She appeared to understand her child's needs better and possess a greater desire and ability to work towards a solution. But I came to recognize a significant defect. It's not as severe and as frightening as Ryan's, but it's present nonetheless. Dyann cares more about Kayla than Ryan does but not anywhere close to as much as she cares for herself.

"I don't condone everything my husband has done. He can be belligerent, he can be tyrannical. But he is a good provider."

"That from an excellent spender."

"And he's taken certain steps I believe to be necessary to ensure our family's safety."

"So you have no qualms with your daughter returning home?"

"Not if she's released into my custody, Your Honor, and my husband is only granted time with Kayla under my supervision."

"That won't work. The only reason Kayla cares to be with my wife is because she knows Dyann can't say no to any request she makes. I want my daughter to become self-sufficient."

"You want to toughen her up all right."

Judge Clemons grabs the back of his head with both hands. I know what he's thinking: *We've been here too many times. All the promises of change, but we always cycle back to the same bad habits. Nothing improves. It's all talk.*

Or maybe that's just what I'm thinking. I like to believe I'm a person who exercises considerable judgment. I like to think I carefully considered Kayla's case before coming to Court. That said, if I were honest, I'd have to admit that when I came here today I intended to recommend Kayla be allowed to return home, but as I get to my feet and brush my skirt to buy a few additional seconds, I realize that's not what I will tell Judge Clemons.

"Your Honor," I begin, taking a few more seconds to be certain where I'm going. "I've carefully reflected on this matter and ... I've come to believe what's in the best interest of Kayla ... would be to place her in another foster home."

I hear others jump to their feet, but I remain focused.

"And I think the family should be one that has raised children who have since left home, preferably to college. A mature couple. Now I know Kayla loves her mother and father and wants to return to them, but I cannot make that recommendation in good conscience."

I hear Ryan and Dyann's voices trying to talk over mine and Q.D. telling them to wait their turn. With my attention diverted by the Harrisons, I come to an abrupt conclusion, unsure of what else I've said and wondering how embarrassing the transcript will read. As I conclude, I observe Judge Clemons holding his gavel aloft and imagine that some NBAer has taken an outside jumper at the buzzer. All eyes in the building are focused on the object. But there is no climactic finish, no scream of excitement, no groans. Judge Clemons gently lowers his hand, and silence descends upon us. I sit, intending to gently tap Kayla's hand but cannot do it.

She runs past me to the podium but turns back my way when she reaches it. "What's love got to do with it?"

I hear Tina Turner's voice.

Kayla shakes her head and addresses Judge Clemons. "That's not why I want to go home. But what other choice do I have? Even if you were to let me go out on my own, you think I'd really be free?"

Kayla stops speaking. I expect her to beg and to make an emotional appeal, but at the age of fourteen she comports herself better than most semi-seasoned lawyers who think more is more when usually it's less.

Judge Clemons leans back in his chair for a moment and closes his eyes. He tilts his head towards the ceiling. After a full minute, he leans towards us.

"I'm not here to judge the totality of anyone's existence. I've seen this family enough to know of its many accomplishments and significant shortcomings. But family law is different than the civil or criminal matters that are tried before me or a jury. There, one side wins, another loses.

"Would that I could make things right, perfect. But I can only rule. Kayla, you're too young to have been taken from your childhood and thrown into the world of adults. And I'm sorry if that world, including yours truly, has failed you. We can only try to do better. And I can only hope that you struggle through no matter where I — with my imperfect vision — send you."

Judge Clemons continues talking and ultimately rules, but I conclude the order is not what's most important. We're all born into families without having been given a choice and forced to make the best of something over which we hold no control. Some are treated better, some worse. Even within a particular family.

I reflect on my childhood when as kids my friends and I would make silly comparisons about the relative talents of our mothers, incomes of our fathers, successes of our siblings. Why did any of that matter? What was the use arguing about who was best?

Ultimately, whether Kayla or my newborn or anyone else succeeds depends far too much on luck. Sure, a few can overcome tremendous obstacles and others can dig their own holes to stumble into. But what's the use of pretending there's any fairness to a farcical system where people start out at different points on the course and the rules can be changed at any point along the way?

Kevin Finnerty received his MFA from Columbia College Chicago. His fiction has appeared in *VLP Journal*, *Blue Lyra Review*, and *Parting Gifts*. He lives and works in the Twin Cities.

After Waking
Ann Hillesland

As soon as Aurora closes her eyes, the falling fear sucks her in: once asleep she won't wake. Her body snaps alert, jolting the bed. Early in their marriage, her husband would roll over and kiss her. "I can always wake you up again," he'd say. Now he's used to the bed quake and doesn't wake.

Aurora has always claimed the hundred years of sleep were dreamless. A lie. The scenes tumble behind her eyelids, still vivid after almost a year—sunset lights pulsing and fading, empty corridors, dark leaves against a dark sky crushing down, trapping her in the bed, clogging her throat. Burying her alive.

In the candlelight (she must always have a candle burning) her husband's chin is prickly. If she leaned over to kiss him now, she'd have to fight her way through the thicket.

She is so tired. Her arms and legs have no strength. She nods off during state dinners. She no longer rides for fear she will fall asleep in the saddle. Would smacking the ground wake her?

Her husband rides to the hunt without her, grasping his bow eagerly as a boy while he paces his horse. Women wave scarves and cheer their young king in the cold morning, breath rising like a magical silver mist. Aurora props herself up against an icy stone wall, feeling decades older than her grinning husband.

At night she rises from her hated bed and wanders the castle, candle in hand. The halls are cold and silent save for snores, as they must have been all those hundred years. But now she's awake. She slips the helmet from a sleeping guard and perches it on a stag trophy head. With the cook snoring near the kitchen fire, she builds a pyramid from the breakfast loaves.

Back in bed, she watches her husband sleep. If he dies before her, will she slip back into the world of endless dreams?

Suits of armor spear apples on their lances, dressmaker's dummies embrace in the ballroom. And still the queen yawns away the days, prowls the halls nightly, waits for sunrise.

One night as she rises, her husband opens his eyes. "Why are you doing it?" he asks, grasping her wrist so she can't leave the bed.

Her hands are shaking. She has not been able to hold them steady for days.

"Do you think it's funny?" he asks. He is not so handsome now, not so charming. Below his bloodshot eyes, a red pillow-fold line slashes across his cheek. His breath smells of onion tart. She would not kiss him awake.

She lies down beside him, in the position she held all those years, hands folded corpse-like on her chest. Her eyes are heavy, but when they close, her mind fills with the old dreams that she is trapped in the bed and will never move again. She gasps alert.

She slips away from her sleeping husband, takes the candle and by its flickering light climbs the stairway she has never, in all her night wanderings, approached. The spiral steps are narrow and shadowed. The bad fairy's curse has lasted longer than the good fairy's. The spindle is still there, needle sharp, ready this time to send her into the dreamless sleep from which she will never have to wake.

Ann Hillesland's work has been published in many literary journals, including *Fourth Genre, Sou'wester, Corium,* and *SmokeLong Quarterly*. It has been selected for the *Wigleaf* Top 50 Very Short Fictions, won the grand prize for prose in a *Spark* contest, and has been presented onstage by Stories On Stage. She is a graduate of the MFA program at Queen's University of Charlotte. For more of her writing, see www.annhillesland.com.

FICTION

Anna Maria Has a Name Like Hills
Elaine Kehoe

She is a collector of names, and this one catches her dreams by the throat, this name on the day's guest roster.

He sits in the alcove between the rocks, watching the moonlight wander over the folding waves. He looks to the sky and gives up the bitterness, makes an offering of it to the moon, and for a fraction thinks he sees it clouding the moon's face, then passing over. For the first time in months he smiles, fully, with his heart. And now, finally, the first line is free to come to him: *She was just one girl, just one in a throng.* The pain of memory begins to transform.

Miranda loves this little alcove in her bedroom, her refuge from the demands of family and business: the bed-and-breakfast guests, the food to prepare, the bedclothes to be washed, the house to be kept clean. Her mother's and aunt's dependence on her.

The moon outside the window pulls her thoughts toward it like the tide. She decides to go for a walk on the beach. There is an alcove there, too, in the rocks. It's like a grotto where a penitent might go to pray, where the moon is a window to heaven, where the mind can wander among the wonders of the world and of God.

The guests have settled in, her mother and aunt gone to bed, the house quiet. But the one name she was most anticipating hasn't been checked off on the roster.

She loves the way she can get inside a name, roll it around in her mind, parse it. She takes them from books, the newspaper, old movies, writes them in a notebook. She especially likes old character actors whose names weren't changed by studios. Akim Tamiroff. S. Z. Sakall. Names with sounds she could feel, that made images. Milo O'Shea, with a skip in the middle like a stone over water. Anna Maria Alberghetti, a name that fell and rose like a range of hills.

Words. During a lonely childhood here by the sea, they kept her company. Poetry and names. If college hadn't been out of her reach, she'd have studied literature.

So she's eager to know what this new guest, this John Keats, is like. *He's probably an auto mechanic or a lawyer,* she thinks. Maybe he never even heard of the poet. She's disappointed at his nonarrival for her own sake, annoyed for her mother's. An empty room.

She picks up a peach from the bowl in the dark dining room and puts it in the pocket of her light summer jacket.

Up here along the coast darkness is rarely completely dense, even away from the house and its porch lights that burn all night. Here the stars seem as close as a ceiling. As a child she would watch and wait for them to fall and bounce on the ground in front of her, so she could chase them like she did fireflies. Here the moon catches itself in the ocean and turns it fluorescent. Her eyes adjust quickly to the outlines of the rocks that string the narrow beach with rough pearls. Her body knows the way. The rocks, the waves, the darkness—they belong to her. The surfers own it in the summer days; in the winter, snowshoers and cross-country skiers, those who come to downhill in the nearby mountains. At night and off-season, this place is hers.

Except that tonight it isn't only hers. She senses it as she approaches the alcove: the presence of someone else. She isn't frightened. The thought excites her.

It's he who starts when she says "hi" in a soft, casual voice, as though they were neighbors meeting on a morning walk.

"Well, hello," he says. "I didn't think I'd meet anyone here."

"Neither did I." He's close in height to her, maybe an inch or two taller. She can't see him well but the outlines of his face and body clarify a little as she looks at him. His face a little round. At first she thinks he's bald, then realizes it's one of those closely shaved cuts that she doesn't like on a man.

She sits on the flat boulder in front of the alcove, sits to one side, giving him room to join her. He does, and neither speaks, two strangers who just happen to sit on the same bench at the bus stop. She takes the peach out of her pocket, starts to move it to her mouth, then stops and offers it to him. He hesitates just a moment, then takes it.

"I like eating peaches down here," she says. "The wetness just seems to go with the ocean."

"A peach on the beach." He smiles. "Do I dare to eat it?"

She regards him through the sides of half-closed eyes. "It's such a sensuous fruit, don't you think? The velvety skin, the soft flesh, the sweet juice, and the hidden pit, like an embryo, inside." He hands it back to her, and she bites out a large, soft, wet chunk. The juice trickles over her lip and down her chin, and she wipes it away with her hand. He's watching her more closely now, and she feels the charge of it.

She holds out her right hand. "Hello, John Keats. We were wondering where you were tonight."

"Ah ha. I thought you just arose from the sea, like Venus. You're from the Alcove, then. Alice Mallon?"

"That would be my mother. I'm Miranda."

Now she can see his grin, wide and white in the moonlight. "'O brave new world that has such people in it.'"

Her laugh is rough, almost mocking. "Oh, now, you can't really be. I mean, I was daydreaming about you being a poet, but I never thought for real. But Shakespeare and Eliot—most people don't quote them when they meet me."

"Well, I'm afraid that's the English teacher in me. I'd give you an A for recognizing the poetry. Were you named for *The Tempest?*"

"No. Miranda was my mother's favorite aunt. But I like to pretend I was." She tosses the peach pit hard and it spans the sand, splashing into the shallow surf.

"How old are you?" The question is sudden and impolite, but she doesn't play at being offended or shrug it off.

"Twenty-four. You?"

"Thirty-three. And I am a complete cliché. A would-be poet, yes. Very much *would be* at this point. That's partly why I'm here. To see if I can take out that 'would.' And yes again, that's my real name. John Jefferson Keats, to be exact. If—when—I write something for public consumption, I'll take out the John. To avoid bad jokes and loathsome comparisons."

"Married?"

He shakes his head.

She smiles an invisible smile, a reverse Cheshire cat.

"Well, Mr. Keats," she stands up and brushes off her jeans. "I guess we'd better get you checked in. The lights went out an hour ago."

He's with the other guests at breakfast. Miranda serves the omelets and vegetable fritters and muffins she's cooked, moving efficiently from kitchen to dining room, friendly to everyone, but always watching him surreptitiously. Her mother and aunt stand at the farmer table in the kitchen, preparing fruit, keeping coffee brewing.

"Mr. Keats would prefer tea," she says, grabbing the large pewter kettle and banging it down on one of the six stove burners.

"He got here awfully late last night," her aunt says. "Where was he, anyway?"

"At the beach. He wanted to see it at night, spend some time alone with it before he came here, into company. He said."

Her mother shakes her head. "Now I've got two dreamers in the house. At least one's only a guest. Here, take these blueberries in."

She's slightly disappointed now that she sees him in the daylight. Now he looks short and boxily built. The buzz cut wasn't so obvious in the darkness, and his face is of only average attractiveness. He isn't her ideal of a poet: the beauty of his namesake, of Shelley or Byron. But he will do for her. She remembers the feeling she got from his body next to hers in the dark.

She's been up since five o'clock, when she drove to the farmer's market for the eggs and fruit. After breakfast she'll clean up the kitchen and dining room, change the linens in all the rooms, do the laundry. She gives the other guests brochures as though handing them their hats, showing them what there is to do in the area. The young couple with two children will be going sailing. The older couple plans to shop in town. As for John Keats—"I'm just going to wander around for a while. Spend some more time by the water." The wide grin again. "Think. Write. I hope." She thinks he's much more attractive when he smiles that way.

Her mother and her aunt will do the afternoon marketing for food for the dinner option offered to guests. The family says they'll be back; the older couple says they'll eat out. She helps make up the shopping list. The family doesn't look gourmet, she tells her mother. Let's stick to plain food this time. Chicken, pasta. That will make things easier and give her more time.

By three o'clock her family has gone. Miranda rushes up to her room on the third floor. She takes a quick shower, then picks out a light soft-cotton tank top and skirt. A hot-day outfit that she doesn't wear often, but it's in the eighties this afternoon. She slips her feet into sandals.

He's there, as she hoped he'd be. She finds him sitting not far from the alcove, closer to the water. The tide is going out and the beach is wider than last night.

"You're not writing." She's disappointed to see that he doesn't have a notebook with him.

"I need to think first. Get it all out in my head."

"Maybe that's why you haven't written much. Keeping it in your head doesn't get it down on paper."

He laughs. "Miranda, are you looking for a job? Muse? Or agent? I could use either."

She sits down on the rock opposite him. "Tell me what's in your head."

"Can't yet. I'll surprise you. I will write it down."

She takes out the two peaches she's brought. "Then tell me why you came here."

She's too intelligent for the looking-for-inspiration-from-the-wild-ocean story, and she senses he knows that. He pauses, staring out over that wild ocean before turning back to her.

"I've left my job."

"You're not going to teach any more? Tired of it? Sick of the kids? Or going to dedicate your life to writing."

"A little of all. And none. Teaching just seemed—too futile now." He pauses, and when she doesn't interrupt, starts again. He's making little circles with his finger in the sand on the rock. "I come from a small town in Massachusetts. Hardesty. No one's ever heard of it. Very self-satisfied place. Happy to be a 'typical New England town.' Mostly white, middle class but gradually climbing toward upper middle. People who worked in the city would move there for their 'quiet retreat.' But during the recession things started to change. People started moving to look for jobs. House prices dropped. Different elements started moving in, and gangs and drugs started to appear in a few areas.

"I had a student from a good family, bright girl, good writer, creative. A teacher's dream. She was so advanced that I started working with her extra time, giving her reading way beyond the class, then discussing it, getting her to do some creative writing. I thought we had a great mentor-protégée relationship.

"One day I was called down to the principal's office. There was a couple I didn't know and two police officers. The couple was glaring at me like I had horns. My student's parents. She'd been out of class for about a week, and I was afraid something was wrong. It was. They had sworn out a warrant for my arrest for inducing a chaste minor to have sex."

He stops. He digs a hole in the sand with his bare toe and puts the peach pit in it.

"She was out of school because she'd had an abortion. She claimed I was the father. Of course I told them it was ridiculous. I was placed on formal suspension. But it seemed they couldn't prove that she'd been 'chaste.' The girl confessed. She was involved with the bad kids, drugs. Got hooked. Slept with her dealer to get the stuff. He was the father."

Miranda closes her eyes.

"She had everything going for her. It made me wonder what was the point of trying to teach literature to kids in a world like this. I'd had enough."

Miranda slips off her sandals and digs her toes into the sand. "What if I'd been your student? Would you have wanted to mentor me? I would've liked that."

"Why do you stay here, Miranda? Did you go to college?"

She shakes her head. "No money for college. And I had to help my mother." She stops, trying to leave the story there, but his eyes are kind and curious. He wants more, and that wanting feels like a drug to her. "The B&B was my father's dream. He put all his savings into it. But he died when I was twelve. My aunt came to live with us then and help with the work, but they're both getting older. They can't handle it all alone."

"But what about your future?"

"I guess this is it. When they pass on—or get too old—I'll take over."

"But you could sell the place. Go to school."

She shakes her head. "It's got two mortgages. There wouldn't be much left. Besides, this is my home. I love it here. I'm used to the work, and I get to meet interesting people." She gives him a deliberately sidelong glance. She hoped to sound matter-of-fact but she's heard the wistfulness in her own voice and hates it that she let him hear it.

He clears his throat once or twice. Then he says, "I'll tell you what I was thinking—what I started to write. In my head."

She sits up, a small anticipatory smile just raising the corner of her lips.

"*Venus Miranda, sea-born, island-bred.*
Did Botticelli dream you, the red
of your hair, your innocent face?
You seem so lonely in this place
Caught between here and nowhere

Your tempest spirit—
"That's as far as I've gotten."
"Thank you," she said.
"Well, it's just a beginning. The start of a draft."

She nods, her eyes down, studying the sand. Then she raises her head and smiles fully at him, and he reels back instinctively, then slowly returns her smile.

The next evening they're both there again, but she carries something with her, more than a peach this time: a kernel of knowledge. They sit within the embrasure of the alcove.

"I found your local paper," she tells him. "I looked it up at the library. It didn't say the same things you said. It didn't say the girl confessed anything. It said you settled out of court and agreed to resign."

His finger trails gently along her arm. "Don't you think I'm innocent?"
"I really don't care."
"No?"
She looks at him. "I'm over twenty-one. I'm not your student."

He gazes back at her; his eyes brighten. A smile grows between them. The walls of the alcove enclose them.

They meet at the alcove when they can: very early in the morning, before her mother and aunt are up, before breakfast, and she runs back to the kitchen, her apron and cooking smells covering, she hopes, the telltale odor of the truth. At night, after dinner, walking to the beach, knowing he will be there. When her mother and aunt both go shopping, he comes to her room, clandestine and the more exciting for it. In between she leaves him to his poetry. He spends days at the beach, even in the rain, protected by the alcove.

When he leaves she feels relieved; his presence was starting to burden her. She wishes him well. He will write, she thinks, become the poet he wants to be.

He'll work at some ordinary job to support himself. He'll marry and maybe divorce, maybe more than once. He won't remember her.

But she will always have this: that she has been a poet's lover. And if he writes a book, she'll frame the cover and hang it on the wall, and show it to all her guests, and say *he's a poet. He spent time here. We were very close.* And the married women will smile and nod, happy that the innkeeper has had her day of passion. They will think her mysterious; keep closer eyes on their husbands while she's around.

And there will be more. She looks at the calendar on the door, where she has marked off the thirty-eight days since he left. She smiles. There will be her son. She knows it will be a son. She'll keep him warm within her over the winter, and he'll warm her, and in the spring he will come, and by the time the gladioli break the surface of the soil she will know him.

He'll have mystery in his life. He'll be the son of a poet, and words will run in his bloodstream. And she, Miranda-of-the-island, will create an alcove for the two of them. She will teach him to love poetry, and he will become a poet of the lusty ocean. And she will name him Keats, because names are words, and words are her magic.

Elaine Kehoe has degrees in English and psychology. She has studied both fiction and creative nonfiction and loves writing that explores the mysteries of the mind and soul and the presence of the transcendent in human life. Her work has also appeared in *Rosebud*, *Word Riot*, *Postcard Poems and Prose*, and *Relief Journal*. She is a freelance copyeditor and lives in Providence, Rhode Island, with her husband and their dog, Honey, the real boss of the house. She is also working on the second draft of a novel and trying to learn to draw. She keeps a sporadic blog at http://elainelk-tealeaves.blogspot.com (but is really a technophobe by nature).

FICTION

Visions
G. Evelyn Lampart

"You have to hide me," I demand. "The Nazis are after me!"

"There are no Nazis here!" Mr. Sender bellows back. He is sitting at the head of his antique dining table. His house is big: three stories high. I once used the bathroom on the second floor, and there were stairs leading higher. There must be an attic.

The group sits around the table watching us. We (five men and I) meet every other week to study *Visions of our Fathers*. We pursue the principles of ethical Judaism. We are Talmudic, dissecting and pondering the maxims of Pirkei Avoth in the original Hebrew. But I have real problems.

Another woman has joined the group tonight. I ignore Sender and introduce myself. She is the rabbi's wife. I welcome her warmly. She readjusts her head scarf, and fumbles with the pages of the text we are about to study. The men sit with lowered eyes.

"Shira!" As Sender addresses me, spittle forms on his mouth. "Sit down!"

"But there *are* Nazis. There are." He doesn't believe me.

Sender glances at the rabbi. Rabbi Klummer appeared a month ago. He insisted that I should not be studying with the men. As an unmarried woman, I was a distraction. But Aaron Susskin advocated for me. To exclude me because I am unmarried, Aaron argued, would be unethical. We were there to learn ethics, not *halachah,* the law, he maintained. They held a vote. The two other men were newly converted, from California. It was three against two. I stayed.

Sender stands and looks down at me. He is tall. I beseech him.

"If the Nazis were chasing me..." I begin again, this time with a supposition. "*Your house should be open*, Sender," I quote. "'*And you should make the poor members of your household.*' We learned this the first week."

He shouts: "*And do not converse excessively with women!*"

That was the end of the passage.

"If someone else was chasing me...?" I give him a loophole.

"Get out. Get out of my house!" Sender points to the door I entered ten minutes earlier.

"I'm not leaving," I threaten. When the Nazis appear I will have nowhere to go, and Sender's house is huge. "Remember the *mitzvah* that says the main thing is doing, not study?" I force the argument. Sender grasps my arm by the elbow, and propels me toward his front door.

"You're touching a woman!" I admonish.

The rabbi does not intervene. He sees the transgression. Rabbi Klummer stands and fingers the black velvet yarmulke covering his head, and heads up the stairs. He leaves behind a tableful of various editions of *Pirkei Avot* decorating a starched white tablecloth.

I don't want to leave. The residential street is far from the subway, and it is dark and cold in December. The Ditmas Park brownstone is warm and well lit. Sender increases the pressure of his hand on my arm. I relax and grow passive. The man rushing me out of his house is strong and could call the police.

Although the streets with abundant trees are poorly lit, I find the subway and sit on a bench waiting for the train going into Manhattan. A man approaches me, breathing heavily. I begin to move away. "*Shira,*" Aaron Susskin says out of breath, and I acknowledge the man in the group who championed my right to study with the men. . "You can come with me," he consoles. "If the Nazis are after you – they are after me too."

I explain to Aaron that my mother is a Nazi.

"So. Your mother." He sighs. "I see. I understand. Of course. My wife is a psychotherapist. And a mother."

My mother put me in a psych hospital after I refused to go on any more blind dates. I went to Rockefeller Center, to the airport at JFK, to the Waldorf Astoria lobby, and to the renovated kitchen of a yeshiva boy who made a pass. I was through with those Jewish boys.

"I have to get married. Or she will have me locked up. Again."

Aaron says that he understands what I went through.

"But it isn't over. She warned me that she can lock me up anytime." I need him to understand completely.

My mother insisted that I keep going out. To keep trying. With a plan to escape, I packed a suitcase with the journals I began when I was *bat mitzvah*. My mother found my work, and threw all of my books into the incinerator. I wailed when I found out. My temple was destroyed. I was bereft with depression and couldn't get out of bed. It was true -- my mother could send me back.

"Did you follow me?" I ask Aaron, relieved that I am not alone. We sit together waiting for the train.

"Sender was wrong to push you away. I was worried for you." He makes it sound so simple.

As simple as the sign I saw on a bulletin board in the Jewish Division of the library in Manhattan advertising a Jewish study group. As simple as my joining with the hope that I would meet intelligent and educated Jews.

"I'm getting off at Seventh Avenue. There are friends in Park Slope..." I mumble. Years ago I had friends. But they left Brooklyn, and I was scared to make the break. "What do you do?" I am curious.

"I'm a business man. In Manhattan." Aaron hands me a business card. "Call me, Shira. I'm not going back there." He twirls his pointer finger around his forehead. "My clinical diagnosis," and he sighs again.

"Seventh Avenue," I announce as we near the station, and get off the train. Aaron waves good-bye. I straighten my back, and head for the street.

On the avenue I pass a familiar looking church, and for the first time in my life I walk up the steps. I want sanctuary. I am tired. There is a bell on the massive wooden door, and I ring it. Again. And again. No one comes to the door. I sit down on the stone steps because it is late. The Nazis would look for me at the study group, but never outside a church.

After working in the field for many years as a clinical social worker, G. Evelyn Lampart gratefully leads an art workshop in a mental health clinic. She is published in *Poetica, Nous, Dirty Chai,* and the anthology *Rozlyn*. She is a lifelong Brooklynite, and has witnessed, and been a part of, its many changes over the years.

NONFICTION

Moonlight Knocking
Mia-Francesca Mcauslan

Woke up with my head in your lap, your arms limp by your sides, the seat too tight. The window was luminous and I thought it was the moon, tapping on the glass. The security guard lowered his torch and moved his arm in a circular motion. Your body, warm beneath my hair, moved too quick and my head thumped onto the seat.

Can't sleep here, he said.

The words must have fumbled around in your French Canadian head, your eyes half-closed, your cock half-hard. I was still lying on the seat with your jacket wrapped around.

The abrupt wake up left no room for softness, for quiet stirrings, and only confirmed the morning as a place of confusion and something like trauma. We crawled out of the car, you and I, into the dawn.

The red station wagon was parked awkwardly in the empty car park. We were in the middle of crossing the Queensland border, flocking towards gentler weather. I was equipped for the unforgiving heat of that summer, my skin lubricated from the tropical sun. Yours was so white from the snow that it shone. In the morning light your rounded shoulders looked like polished stones.

We walked to the edge of the car park at the bottom of the lighthouse. The ocean was brimming beneath us. So calm it could melt. Your eyes so grey they leaked. The security guard lingering in shadows, shining torches in the windows of vacant cars. The sound of frightened 'roos scattering leaves. Eventually he must have gone.

We sat there on a wooden bench drifting between awake and asleep while I dreamt of my childhood. I had memories of my mother behind the wheel of a car, my sister asleep in the back. Parked in different streets, police always knocking on the window. We moved like nomads through the night. The rainwater sloshing around our ankles, we slept with our feet up on the seats. I heard my mother humming in that dreamlike state, her eyes so red. There is no peaceful sleep inside a car. There is only a place between rest and awake, something that the body does and has to do.

We sat there until the sun came up and for a few hours after that. In your own language you whispered over and over again:

Today my love the leaves are thrashing against the wind.

(*Aujourd'hui mon amour les feuilles s'envolent au vent*)

I tried to wrap my mouth around the oval sounds the same way you did but my lips were too loose. We cooked beans on the gas stove. We lay on the patchy grass. Our backs twisted from the embrace, stiff from the night and the galas calling to each other, pink like the sky. We walked back to the car, the tar so hot it stuck to our shoes, and I slept all the way to Port Macquarie.

POETRY

Forgotten Coast River Ark
Karla Linn Merrifield

On the day of many pairings
of a set piece placed au natural
on the primordial stage
are lines that do accommodate:
cotton mouth and cotton mouse.

A nine-time Pushcart-Prize nominee and National Park Artist-in-Residence, Karla Linn Merrifield has had over 500 poems appear in dozens of journals and anthologies. She has eleven books to her credit, the newest of which is *Bunchberries, More Poems of Canada*, a sequel to *Godwit: Poems of Canada* (FootHills Publishing), which received the Eiseman Award for Poetry. She is assistant editor and poetry book reviewer for *The Centrifugal Eye*, a member of the board of directors of Just Poets (Rochester, NY), and a member of the New Mexico State Poetry Society, the Florida State Poetry Society and TallGrass Writers Guild. Visit her blog, Vagabond Poet, at http://karlalinn.blogspot.com.

FICTION

Second Thoughts
Lynsey Morandin

It's not until the fourth or fifth time that I finally realize something's wrong.

I walk through our front door and am immediately greeted by green walls. "Mint," my wife says, knowing I wouldn't identify the correct shade on my own. The walls had been blue when I left that morning. And lilac and grey and beige before that.

"What do you think?" she asks, kissing me on the cheek and beaming as her eyes bounce from me to her new project and back again. *Maybe this is it*, I think. *She looks happy; maybe this is the last time.*

"I love it," I say. "It's the best one yet, for sure." I smile wide with my teeth to hide the fact that I'd say anything at this point to get her to stop. She smiles back.

"Oh, thank God!" she says. "I was worried you'd hate it. But I think it'll go great with those yellow chairs."

"Definitely. And now we can finally put all our frames up."

By now she's shuffling me over to the table where dinner is waiting. She dishes veggies onto my plate as she tells me about her trip to the hardware store in search of the perfect color to drench our new apartment in. I laugh when it's appropriate, smile and nod and feign shock, but my eyes keep darting toward the very impressive pyramid of paint cans taking up residence on our balcony. *One, two, three, four*, I count. Five. Five cans of paint. Five different colors in just a week.

She chats animatedly about the phone call she had with her mother back home, how they've gotten six feet of snow already and all of the trees are falling under the weight of the ice.

"It must look so beautiful," she says. "Of course they'd get snow like that as soon as I leave."

I hesitate, trying to read her expression. "Do you want to go back for a visit?"

She snorts out a laugh. "No, baby. We just got here!"

As I'm tidying up after dinner, I catch her staring at the new walls of our living room. In the low light of evening, the color leeches into her face, coating her and giving her a sickly air. Suddenly she looks back at me accusingly, then smiles.

"How about a movie?" she asks.

"Sure."

She takes on the job of picking the perfect one and I finish up with the dishes. From this angle I can see that she isn't looking right at the TV, that her eyes are aimed just a little too high and that her thumb is resting on the button but isn't pushing it. I wash the last spoon over and over again, my fingers wrinkling until I lose feeling in them.

Fifteen minutes later I walk over to the couch and find her in front of the TV, the guide set to channel 2.

"Did you find one?" I ask.

She jumps slightly. "Oh, sorry. I wasn't even paying attention. Lost in my thoughts, I guess."

I sit down next to her and we choose a movie together, some comedy she's seen a thousand times. But she doesn't laugh when she should, she doesn't cry when she usually does. And I can't help but notice how the TV reflects its light onto our mint walls and I pull her in a little closer.

I wake up on the couch, my back aching and the credits rolling on the TV. My wife is standing beside the television, arms gripping her robe tight to her body and feet sunken into a deep imprint in the plush carpet. She runs one hand along the wall in the light cast from a nearby lamp and looks more puzzled than I've ever seen her.

"Are you alright?" I ask. She ignores my question.

"I hadn't thought about what this color would look like in this light." Her eyes dart toward me and then quickly back to the wall. "It looks so good in sunlight, but it looks completely different now."

I pull myself off the couch and make my way over to her as she turns the lamp on and off repeatedly. I lean in and kiss her forehead; I don't think she registers it. "I don't know," I say, "I kind of like it."

"Kind of? Is that how you want to live? *Kind of* being happy?" The color of her eyes gets lost in the dark and she stares up at me through black voids. "That's not good enough for me," she says, her words piercing my skin. Then she looks away from me, first at the floor and then back to that goddamn wall.

"I'll just repaint it tomorrow."

"You've been painting all week, honey," I venture. I place a hand lightly on her shoulder. "Why don't you go out tomorrow? Get some sun? You can check out some of the tourist things to do."

She whips around so fast that I pull my arm away as a reflex. I think she's looking at me, but I can't tell in the dark. "I'm not a tourist," she says. "I live here."

She pads back down the hallway and into our bedroom, leaving me behind.

By morning she decides she wants yellow, and by the time I leave for work it's red. Like her room back home, she says. She texts me during my lunch break to see if I think it's a good idea to just do grey again, the one she originally said made our apartment feel like a graveyard. She's reconsidering it, she says. And it would be easy to match.

At $50 a can, her new project is getting expensive. I pick up overtime, telling myself I'll do whatever I can to be able to afford all the paint she wants, that she deserves to be happy and that eventually she will be. That after a while she'll finally feel at home.

But that's not the truth. Not all of it.

I sit at my desk, watching as everyone around me packs up and heads toward the door, leaving another workday behind and rushing home to their families. I overhear them talking about how taxing it is to work in a cubicle all day, how easy it is to lose your mind staring at those walls. My eyes lock on the expanse of beige in front of me, and all I can think of is oatmeal: its warmth, its comfort.

I'm startled out of my daydream when a co-worker leans into my cubicle and says "Workin' hard?" I smile back at him, vaguely mention something about reports. He nods and puts his jacket on, and I realize it's 5:30.

I text my wife to say I'm going to be late, that the boss needs me to stay. Then I grab some pins from the supply closet and tack a photo to the wall. I can't help but mimic the smile I hold in the photograph, staring into the camera next to my brother. I pin up another of a vacation to the Grand Canyon, and another from my mother's birthday.

I don't leave until 7:00.

In the car, my hands tighten around the wheel and my stomach clenches with every mile. I picture another new color on the walls, yesterday's shade still speckled on my wife's eyebrow. On the surface she shows joy. Manufactured satisfaction.

In my head I replay all the conversations we'd had before moving here. *I don't care where we are*, she says. *Let's start over somewhere far away. I think a change would be good.*

I stand in front of our door, my hand hanging in mid-air as I reach for the doorknob. But I can't turn it. I can't bring myself to walk in and stand face-to-face with another color, whatever it is; in red I see her anger, in blue, her tears. In grey I just see her giving up.

Today's new hue will break my heart. With every coat of paint, I lose my grip on the thought that these walls, that color, this home will ever be enough for her. That I will ever be enough for her.

Through the door I swear I hear the squeak of our ladder, her soft steps as she climbs each rung. My arm falls back down to my side and I walk quietly back to the car.

Lynsey Morandin is your typical writer/editor: drinks too much, works too little, has a cat. She moved from Canada to Alabama for love and now co-runs a small press and literary magazine called *Hypertrophic*. She hates flying, can never get enough coffee, and is desperate to see the Toronto Maple Leafs win the Stanley Cup in her lifetime. You can find some of her work in places like *The Southern Tablet* and *That Lit Site*, or learn more about her press at www.hypertrophicpress.com.

Riverside Living
Roisín O'Donnell

Baby's breath, I think it's called. That antique lace of blossoms under which they've built a nest. They have a right. No one ever asked them how they were planning to finance it. Or investigated their credit history. The things they've used are gnarled and sharp. Brittle grass, snapped reeds and wiry moss. Splintered twigs and saxifrage. Raspy-edged Alder leaves. And yet their nest looks soft. And she, head tucked under a night-fluttered wing, looks even softer. She has a right. No one ever asked her if she was entitled to maternity leave. If her job was stable. Or what she was planning to do about day-care. No one ever glanced to her webbed feet for a ring. And he. Cruising in golden evening light, his long neck gilded to a regal hue. Circling the dark wind-furrowed water, never drifting far from where she sleeps. His jet eyes scan the river bank, his dripping beak held high. He has a right. No one ever questioned his intentions. Or asked if he had health insurance. Or how he planned to support a family. Together, they wait. Her white body compassed by a mossy halo. Calm. Composed. Reflections rippling. A postcard of serene. But heaven help any wildling fox that ventures from the undergrowth. Any misdirected mallard. Any creeping water vole. They've built a nest. They have a right. They will hiss through razor teeth that snap and slice. Wings will spread. And arch. And rise. And rise.

Roisín O'Donnell lives in Dublin, with family roots in Derry. Writing since a young age, her stories and poems have been published in journals internationally. Her work features in *Young Irelanders*, and in the award-winning anthology of Irish women's writing *The Long Gaze Back*. Nominated for a Pushcart Prize and the Forward Prize, she has been shortlisted for several international writing awards, including the Cúirt New Writing Prize and the Wasafiri New Writing Prize. She has received honorary mentions in the Bath Short Story Award and the Fish Flash Fiction Prize and was a prize winner in the Carried in Waves radio competition. She is the current recipient of a literature bursary from the Arts Council of Ireland. Her debut short story collection "Wild Quiet" will be published by New Island Books in spring 2016.

That Scene in "Jaws"
Joseph Nieves

When Hooper's gruesome vessel
emerges from the churning, open ocean,
all mangled aluminum–
That's what your bicycle looked like,
twisting out the trunk
of your friend's car
in the hospital parking lot.
I saw like Chief Brody did,
guts wrenched.
Inside, you're in a hospital bed,
scared. You don't remember
what happened, but I picture the whip
of soft hair on steel panels.
Hear the smack of skull on street.
Your bike somersaulting
behind you. The hushed
oh-my-gods of witnesses.
Later, I'll wonder
what I'd do without you
and contemplate
the stages of grieving.
Now, I say I like your neck brace
and think about how much cleaner
hospitals appear on tv.
This doesn't look like a place
where people get better.
I work at distraction

while the doodads blink and bloop,
and we put on this dress rehearsal
for a scene like this
we'll play out many years from now.
We might switch roles. Or maybe,
if it serves the story, we'll give my lines
to someone else, and split
your part into two.

Joseph Nieves is an undergraduate studying creative writing at Westminster College in Fulton, Missouri. His work has appeared online at *The Molotov Cocktail* and on his mother's refrigerator.

POETRY

Appetite
Keli Osborn

Until I gave up sharp cheeses
and crimson wine from the bottom
of a green bottle, I didn't know
what I wanted. When the doctor
took away biscuits, I freely smeared
soft butter on my calloused feet.

An allergist blacklisted durum,
and I built spaghetti birdcages
for all of my gluttonous friends.
When a healer asked me to bypass
almonds and sunflower seeds,
I buried granola beneath the roses.
How I miss the air of whipped cream,
sweet tang and drizzle of balsamic.

Packing forbidden scrambled eggs
around crystal and silver, I ship
longing and soup spoons to a future
in which the costliest shawls remain
those woven from the fine beard hairs
of wild ibex. Silence hugging
my shoulders is more than absence
of sound, cravings other than want.

I think it was John Cage who muted
instruments for a four-minute piece:
strings and winds, black and white keys,
all stilled. I might hear a world in quiet,
surrender desire to sated composition—
set a place at the table for this abundance.

Keli Osborn lives in Eugene, Oregon. Her poems have appeared or are forthcoming in *Verseweavers, Allegro, KYSO Flash,* and *Dona Nobis Pacem*—an anthology from the Lane Literary Guild. Formerly a newspaper reporter, manager in local government and university instructor, Keli recently has explored the Italian language, belly dancing and comedy improv.

FICTION

Trappings
Melissa Ostrom

During the open house, Meg performed like a hostess forced to entertain guests she'd never invited, opening the front door, ostensibly in welcome, but inwardly seething, *Go away*. She could hardly believe the strangers peeking in her pantry, examining her bedroom closet, experimentally stepping into her glass-walled shower. She could barely tolerate the impudence.

Yes, she and Jim had agreed putting the house up for sale made sense. It would simplify the splitting of their assets. Ease the business of starting over. But as soon as the first stranger patted her refrigerator and asked if the appliances would be included in the purchase, Meg realized she didn't want to sell. Simply couldn't. So after the open house, during the subsequent house viewings, she began to quietly sabotage the selling process in small ways, ignoring the realtor's cheery suggestions: flowers, freshly baked cookies, a picture for the second floor hallway's bare wall. She didn't mow, clean, air, or spruce.

But still, the Langdons, newlyweds, scheduled a second visit. Then another.

Meg dreaded the implications. Instead of leaving the third tour to the realtor, as he firmly recommended, she remained in the house and shadowed the young couple, skulking into the rooms (Jan's old room, Linnie's, petite spaces that, though long since emptied of posters, perfumes, and trinkets, somehow still contained them) before trailing the Langdons down to the kitchen, as helpless as a wave-washed pebble, caught, drowned, lost in the undertow of their interest.

The day suited her foreboding, gray and intermittently wet. She wanted these newlyweds to peer out back, so they'd discover how the low-lying yard held the rain like a sink and guess at the mosquitoes that would breed in such muck and see how all the bushes needed trimming. Perhaps they'd even note the broken latch on the screen door. Meg had willfully neglected the small repairs. She wished she had more to brandish.

Then twenty minutes into the visit, the great room suddenly drummed a wet noise, interrupting the realtor's praise for the cherry cabinetry.

A leak! Meg rejoiced.

All four crossed the room to inspect the ceiling.

More than the drip's occurrence suggested divine assistance. So did its location. The plopping should have happened upstairs, closer to the roof, rather than spanning the great room corner, traveling from the ceiling to the pine floor, past the wall-sized bookcase of crammed volumes.

It fell singly and straight like a determined pilgrimage, like a searching finger, grazing spines, *Master and Margarita*, *Moon-Spinners*, *Corelli's Mandolin*, *Nightingale Wood*, *Strange Music*, and more, some of the dampened titles belonging to Jim, others to Meg, the entire collection soon to be divided, boxed, shelved elsewhere. Maybe read by another.

The patter continued, an erratic heartbeat, the strange drumming of a holy ritual, summoning for Meg remembrances: reading in bed beside Jim, shopping with him and the girls at the used bookstore, reading chapters aloud on long trips, swapping favorite novels, scorning the disappointments.

While the realtor soothed the prospective buyers' concerns about wood rot and promised to get someone over, right away, to take care of the problem, Meg stood silently. And still, moments later, after he'd escorted the Langdons out, she remained in the corner, striving to recall where she was and who she was for each book, the versions of herself she'd abandoned, the selves she could no longer manifest, even if she tried. So much of what she'd held, ached for, treasured, and fed had departed too, long before this purl began to sound, again and again, on the wide plank floor, trilling the grain, pooling on knots.

Melissa Ostrom lives in rural western New York with her husband and children. She serves as a public school curriculum consultant, teaches English at Genesee Community College, and writes whenever and however much her five-year-old and six-year-old let her. Her work has appeared in *Lunch Ticket*, *Thrice Fiction*, *Oblong*, *decomP*, *Monkeybicycle*, and elsewhere.

POETRY

After-Images
Alyse Richmond

Clutching the railing, I squint, induce
a headache. There it is –
The strangest blue whipping
lines through the Wadden like after-
images of a sparkler; an electric
jellyfish. I want to paddle
alongside, trace its willy-nilly path.
But I watch it fade
into a fog, and descend into the cabin
where cards are being thrown,
where bottles of Shiraz and Hertog Jan
are being emptied, voices
swelling with the returning tide.

Alyse Richmond currently resides in Pittsburgh, Pennsylvania, and is in the process of completing an M.F.A. in creative writing at Chatham University with concentrations in poetry, publishing, and travel writing. Her work has been featured in *Welter, The Lincoln Underground, The Doctor T.J. Eckleburg Review, The Found Poetry Review, Lines + Stars, Helix Magazine* and *El Portal*, among others.

Numerical Happenstance
Ruth Sabath-Rosenthal

Body chilled by years of neglect,
my twin lies in a hospital bed

trying to grasp how she's come
to this. The sum of my fears,

she's the one person I dread
I could be, save for some kink

in our link of genetic fiber.
Struggling not to catch her death

of cold, I've steered clear of her
notion that our birth was not just

numerical happenstance. Yet,
at times, I find myself more

akin to that concept than sanity
permits, & though I fall into

the black hole of her undoing,
so far I've managed to climb back

out & into the asylum of my life.
Out, according to my twin,

the same way I exited the womb,
climbing over her in order to be first.

Ruth Sabath-Rosenthal is a New York poet, well-published in literary journals and poetry anthologies throughout the U.S. and internationally. In October 2006, her poem "on yet another birthday" was nominated for a Pushcart Prize. Ruth has authored 5 books of poetry: *Facing Home* (a chapbook), *Facing Home and Beyond*, *little, but by no means small*, *Food: Nature vs Nurture*, and *Gone, but Not Easily Forgotten*. For more about Ruth, please feel free to visit her website: www.newyorkcitypoet.com.

FICTION

Clean Dogs
Matthew Walsh

The day would start with me in the passenger seat, lapping up oatmeal and fresh cut strawberries with vanilla soy milk. My partner, Michael, and I would drive through Guelph until we reached work just outside Fennel, Ontario, where he was a laboratory assistant and I was a dog cleaner at a dog food testing facility. We worked and lived together, and it worked for a while. Evenings we'd just do our own thing, sometimes one of us would go out, the other would stay home. For me the dog food job was supposed to be temporary.

I had had two jobs, the morning job cleaning shit and an evening job at a restaurant where I microwaved frozen curries. Michael hated his job but it paid. He hated grinding their poop and weighing poop and then checking the nutritional value in poop. I managed a whole wall of microwaves, to be exact. The restaurant, Curry in A Hurry, fired me when they found out where I worked in the morning. I probably was going to bring them parasites, they said. They didn't want anyone to make the connection between the guy who cleaned up dog crap and the guy who heated up curry.

The facility was beginning to make a lot of money and there was a rumor about expansion, extending the dog halls so the facility could do more dog food testing trials and increase revenue. The new dogs, I heard, would be mixed breeds, possibly temperamental, larger than the beagles, less docile. There was a barn being built on the property that would have six extra rooms, but it wasn't ready for life just yet.

Every day, I put the dogs outside in their designated groups while I pressure-washed their room. When that was done, I would let the dogs back inside, put them in their cages and feed them two types of food, Trial A and Trial B, noting which one the dog ate out of first.

It sounded easy if you leave out the fact that when the lights went on in the morning, the dogs would howl, and it would be awful, so awful the dog cleaners needed ear protection.

I would walk in to greet the dogs, check for any eye infections, scratches, signs of soreness, blood, all while they hid at the back of their paddocks or jumped furiously against their cage door, flinging a confetti of shit and kibble at me. The scared ones were the cutest. They didn't do anything but avoid you, and ran out of the room when you needed them to.

The dog rooms were a robin's egg blue color, with a drainage system running along the wall. Once you power-washed the rooms clean, the drainage system took all the shit and old food away to a septic tank just north of the complex in the middle of a field.

In the field was a pond where there were other signs of life. Frogs had their babies in the pond in the spring and by summer there were plenty of frogs living there in the muck. One year this didn't happen, and the next year, the number of frogs died down. Either raccoons ate them, or the dogs did, or they died because the water sources around the building were too polluted.

You couldn't drink the water there—even if it was filtered. Every cleaning supply we used, the orange tile cleaner, dog shampoo soap, descaler, went into the ground. Cleaning chemicals, feces both human and canine, you name it. I poured water from the tap one day and my Michael swatted a glass out of my hand. Even if the water was boiled, Michael said, no one should drink it. My first week there, I couldn't eat because anything exposed to the air in my mind had been contaminated, but I eventually broke down. I started covering my Tim Hortons coffee with a piece of paper, and if that didn't work, I'd just pick dog hair off the cup rim before I took a drink.

All summer the hallways were littered with horse flies. They would crawl all over the windows like TV static, buzz by my ears. There would be flies everywhere you needed to put your hand. Door knobs, your pen, the clipboard, the dog brush, on the toilet seat.

Every morning there would be a pile of maggots in at least one of my rooms feeding on the dog shit. Maggots would crawl back out of the drain once they'd been blasted away, little black beetles would hide in the corners of the room, small as watermelon seeds.

I would let the dogs out and stand at the back of my room with the power washer and spray down the bars of the cages, the back walls, making sure all the shit and food went into the drains. Each week we'd have to take an orange cleaner and brush down the floors and walls just to take the sanitation to another level, removing decalcified piss and shit stains, killing any microscopic parasites. The orange cleaner burned my lungs, and if anyone got it in their eye, the cleaner would burn their cornea. Somehow the orange cleaner got in one of my co-worker's eye and she had to wear an eye patch over it, and when it was removed she had only recovered partial vision.

Once in a while you worked with someone else, but usually I was by myself. Sometimes a dog was too old or injured to go outside with a group, so it would stay inside with me while I cleaned. I wasn't getting along at home with Michael and coming to work was depressing. I let one dog stay in with me when I cleaned. She liked to sit by my legs while I power-washed and I'd try not to trip on her.

Her name was Clarice, and she was a fat, squat little beagle with two back legs that could no longer support her. When she sat down her legs looked like rubber chickens, but Clarice was a favorite of mine. I would put her on a leash after her room was cleaned, brush her fur and chop her nails off. None of the dogs liked getting their nails chopped, but Clarice couldn't feel her back legs, so she was content with what was happening to them. She would sit with her back legs folded under her, sticking out at impossible angles. Everyone in the dog hall knew she had to be reported but no one wanted to be the person to do it.

When she was given her pain meds in a meatball of wet food, I took her for walks past the water cooler, kitchen, and laboratory where Michael grinded and analyzed dog poo. I tried giving Clarice as much attention as possible one day. The veterinarian stopped me. "Is she still eating?" they asked me, and I said yes.

It was dangerous to say *No, they weren't eating.* If the dogs weren't eating then they weren't valuable. I heard rumors about what happened to the dogs if they didn't eat, but I hadn't actually *seen* anything awful happen to any dog. Despite the fact that a dog's sole purpose there was to test different dog foods, they got outside every day, got baths on a monthly rotating basis and had better vet care than most household pets. Clarice didn't have a bad life. She lived like a millionaire. She never had to worry about anything. Stuff was just handed to her.

One morning, Michael and I were late for work. We were fighting about oatmeal and trying to get out of the house on time. He was going to leave me, he said, one day. One day he almost did. Driving into Fennel, Michael accelerated the car in anger, passed the big Walmart that was being built across from a graveyard, and a cop car pulled up out of nowhere. He didn't give Michael any warning or sympathy, and when we got ticketed, Michael said, "You're paying the ticket, it was your fault."

"How is it my fault? You were driving." I put my empty oatmeal bowl under the car seat. We were fighting because I couldn't leave the house without the oatmeal. I had to eat something. Oatmeal only took five minutes. Breakfast was important. If I didn't have it I wouldn't survive the day at work. He didn't understand because all he did was grind up poop all day and run tests. He wasn't lifting up dogs and breaking up the occasional fight or reporting face cancers to the vet. I needed energy. I didn't want to waste it fighting with him.

When we pulled up late, the smokers outside buzzed with news that new puppies were coming. A new generation of dogs. I wondered how many puppies were coming. I didn't see room for any more dogs, except for the barn, and that wasn't ready yet. The running water needed to be hooked up.

I took off my outside clothes and changed into my coveralls and rubber boots. My partner had already changed and was in the laboratory looking into a microscope while a poop solution boiled in a beaker beside him. I decided I wouldn't look at him all day, and he decided when they went to Tim Hortons he wouldn't tell me.

I walked to my hallway and flicked on the lights in my three rooms, and the dogs howled as usual. In the first room I let out all the off-leash dogs into the field, and put the groups into their paddocks. I gathered up all the used dishes and took them to the kitchen, trying not to think about the ticket we had got. I asked one of the kitchen people about the puppies that were coming. "They aren't coming yet! Not until the new barn is built and that won't be for months," a woman named Arlene said. "A lot of changes coming."

There were rumors about expanding but no one knew when it would happen. This business needed eaters and space. Space was important, you couldn't just pack as many dogs as you wanted into one room or they'd fight. I walked past the laboratory room and Michael was drinking an extra large Tim Hortons coffee. I wouldn't even look at him. I was already on my last room— Clarice's room— two hours before my day was finished. After her room was cleaned I took her for a walk around the facility, slowly, as slow as she wanted to go. We made it halfway through the kitchen, past the lab, and we were on our way back to her room when the veterinarian stopped us to look at her feet.

"Have you reported this weakness to the dog supervisor?" she asked. Her name was Colleen.

I nodded. "Everyone seems to know about it," I said.

"Will you bring her into the treatment lab for me?" Colleen asked, "and put her on the examining table?"

I walked the dog towards the treatment room, watching Michael boil another beaker of shit.

Sometimes I did work socializing the male dogs, or slept in the break room until Michael came and kicked my chair telling me it was time to go home. The next day, in the afternoon, when I was waiting for him, I decided to take Clarice out to the field but she wasn't in her room.

Clarice could have still been with Colleen. I didn't think anything of it until the final room was cleaned and the dogs were back in their paddocks. I went to the kitchen and asked Arlene where Clarice's dish was. "She's in the vet lab and that's where she's eating," Arlene said.

I peeked my head in the window of the vet lab, and Clarice was sitting on a table chewing a milk bone. She had a pink blanket wrapped around her back legs. The vet came into the main room from the supply closet and caught me looking in, so I opened the door. "I was just looking for this dog."

"You know that you're supposed to report ailments to the vets, right?"

"Ailments?" I asked. Clarice had been walking like that since I had started work there and the vet knew it.

"This dog can't walk. I'm calling in Becky to come look at her."

Becky was the owner, and when the vet said the dog wouldn't be coming back to the room today I figured Clarice would be back tomorrow. In the car on the way home I told Michael about Colleen.

"They are starting to phase out all the old dogs," Michael said, turning up the radio, "so don't be surprised when we lose a few."

The next day there was a memo about reporting any ailment whether it was serious or mild in an attempt to better monitor animal health. Most of the cleaners thought this was a bad idea because it meant more work for them, but I knew it was just a way for the vets to decide which dogs were good eaters and which weren't before the new puppies arrived.

Colleen was in Clarice's room when I came in the next morning, oatmeal-less. She didn't say anything to me, but took Clarice away. I started with that room since I was already in it. I put the dogs out, cleaned, and did it two more times. It was only one in the afternoon. Michael wouldn't be done until four. I went and ate lunch in the break room.

If I had this much time left over, it was off the clock, because dog cleaners got paid for only so many hours. I walked all the aggressive male dogs who led me on the leash across the field, to the pond where they would look down, maybe for other signs of animal life. That day was overcast, grey, the air was wet. Bumblebees trailed from flower to flower in the field. No flowers grew in the one metre radius around the building, but further out they did: purple blossoms, dandelions, little white flowers I thought were baby's breath. When Michael was done he called out to me from the back door of the facility. He was still in his work clothes, and he waved to me. I got up off the grass and walked the dog, Rocky, to his cage. Rocky had a brother, Bullwinkle, once that I never met. Apparently they were exactly alike, mostly brown with a white bib, white socks, and a violent tendency to bite.

I got changed, put my stuff in a locker and met Michael in the car. I thought we'd talk about the speeding ticket but we didn't say anything. I fell asleep and when I woke up Michael was getting his stuff out of the car. I picked up my bowl from under the seat. In the elevator Michael just stared at the bowl, not saying anything. "They put a lot of the older dogs to sleep today," Michael said when we got to our floor.

"It seems so sad. I don't know why they can't take them to a farm to die."

"They're lab dogs. They have no immune systems for the outside world," Michael said, unlocking the front door. We dropped our stuff by the door, kicked our shoes off.

"They're going to put Clarice down soon. I know it. She wasn't in her room," I said, putting my oatmeal bowl in the sink.

"They put her down this afternoon," Michael said, drinking from a two liter of coke and wiping his lips.

"Why didn't anyone tell me?" Had they really killed one of my dogs without telling me? Would dogs just be there one day and then gone the next? I thought about Clarice and her screwed up legs.

Michael took another drink from the two liter. "They don't tell you, they just take them."

"That's awful. What if we wanted to say goodbye?" I went to the bedroom and took off my clothes.

Michael leaned against the doorframe, eating out of a bag of chips. "Do you want to go somewhere for supper?"

"Where?" I grabbed a towel from the closet. I was hungry and mad at my job. Feeding those dogs just to lead them to their deaths. There were so many old dogs there, so expect a few changes coming. Hadn't someone said that to me? I showered, cleaning under my nails, my hair, beard. I soaped myself up twice, brushed my teeth twice. I toweled off and got dressed. We went to dinner at Thai Elephant, eating quietly at a corner table. Why didn't Michael come and get me? I wanted to know but I didn't ask. He slurped Pad Thai into his mouth.

In the morning we left together, and in Clarice cage was another dog, a cute, smaller dog named Gumdrop. Gumdrop went out with the other female dogs. I cleaned the room, washed all the maggots down the drain, and put Gumdrop and the other dogs into their cages. When the dog food dishes were dropped in their cages I noted which bowl they liked more than the other, and moved on to the next one, then the next one, wondering if the empty cages when I walked into the rooms meant that someone else had left me.

Matthew Walsh is a poet and short story writer whose work has been featured in *Geist Online, Matrix, Joyland, Descant, Arc Poetry, Zaum, Hoax,* and *the Fractured Nuance.* You can reach him on Twitter at @croonjuice.

POETRY

Pink
Scott Wordsman

A red Honda Civic is straddling the bisecting line
of highway forty-six west, swerving over the teeth
of the road's white zipper. The sky is bright
this morning but no driver with a proper pair

of shades or a sun visor should have a problem
staying in just one lane. You are late to work
but would rather apologize for it later than have
your wing mirror clipped off by this swaying sedan.

While you are not a person swayed by stereotypes,
you need to know the demographic of the driver;
sometimes it is reassuring to see if your assumptions
are correct. As you prepare for this pursuit, a cobalt

Camry appears on your right. You try to meet eyes
with its driver, as if to say, What the hell is going on
up there, but she is a beast of a woman looking straight
into the feedbag on her lap and it makes you want

to cry but you sit up straight and bash your fist
against the horn as if one strident sound could shake
the planet into consciousness, but it can't and nothing
changes. You begin to see the Civic as a rival

from your past, the taunting you recall turns to hatred
and seeps into your spit, when you bite down on your lip
the blood you breathe mixes with the gum you are chewing
and where are the police to pull these lunatics over?

Your armpits have fused with your sleeves and sweat
has stained the air, you roll down the window to a road
that smells like piss and rain, this spring has been warm
and awful, your daughter is fifteen and thinks

you are coming on to her when suggesting going out
for ice cream alone as you can't stand the thought
of your wife beating you over the brain for choosing
a large cone over a small cup because what other

indulgences do you have left to own? You decide
to pass the Civic on the shoulder. Who would receive
a ticket first, you think, then ask, Can cops multitask
like that? So as you lay on the gas you catch a glimpse

of her there, the bob of brownish hair, some frays
of pink near the ends, a teenaged mess and you do not
understand why she is screaming nor who her sentiments
are geared toward but as you neck yourself nearer

you notice her phone propped up on the dash and how
she is a violent cryer, a cockpit sobber, with one hand
to her temple, the other flimsy, fingering the wheel.
You want to strangle her and you want to swaddle

and assure her that no matter who is on the other end
he is not worth dying for on a Tuesday morning
between Bloomfield and Paterson. Yet from watching
this display, you begin to taste the tang of jealousy

swirling inside your head, for you have never been
as intoxicated by someone's words as she, so much so
that you would risk it all, especially before lunch;
and while you recognize this selfish sense of the world

to be characteristic of her age, you know you would trade
your summer months and pension to be that foolish again,
to crash your car for anyone who could rescue you from
your insignificance, even for a minute, but the notion

slips as you speed by her on the left to where you keep
on driving till you notice that her car has disappeared
down an exit and you do not think of her again until
three years later when your daughter dyes her hair

pink one evening and you eat just as much dessert
as you would and start to wonder if anything else
will feel the same, but it ends there. In any event,
you're not the type of person to lose sleep over these things.

Scott Wordsman is an MFA candidate at William Paterson University. His poems have appeared or are forthcoming in *The Puritan, Slipstream Press, The Main Street Rag,* and others. He lives in New Jersey.

Trial & Error

"Action and reaction, ebb and flow, trial and error, change—
this is the rhythm of living."

— Bruce Barton

POETRY

I stare down ash
E. Kristin Anderson

I stare down   ash—
    this is where I
  was   bricks, collapsed,
a charred   point of reference for
    myself in this sea of
     almost a month.
        The coal justice
    escaped the why.   Perhaps
anyone would have the odd
     condition of
       returning.
But no one is returning
  and   against my venture,
    invisible,   circling—
     there's no intelligence.
  I had to see   so much.   I made it
    their plans,
  finally
    organized.   His hands
let go.   A day, a little tour
      is just
   the same.
   The same.   My left temple
hit me with the coil. Memories swirl,
try to sort out   what is false

                    in the ruins:
         This hard concussion?
                    still
           the drugs,   my sometimes guess.
I'm still convinced that hallucinating
         snakes
                 (one of the
                         simplest things)
              begins in my home.
I was   the hunger. I
         was
dead—likely,   probably   dead.
              Should I come down?
My voice reaches   through the watching,
         crouched down,
                 elbows on my thighs,   braced.

   This is an erasure poem. Source Material: Collins, Suzanne. *Mockingjay*. New York: Scholastic, 2014. 3-4. Print.

E. Kristin Anderson is a Pushcart nominated poet and author who grew up in Westbrook, Maine, and is a graduate of Connecticut College. She has a fancy diploma that says "B.A. in Classics," which makes her sound smart but has not helped her get any jobs in Ancient Rome. Kristin is the co-editor of *Dear Teen Me*, an anthology based on the popular website. Her YA memoir *The Summer of Unraveling* is forthcoming in 2017 from ELJ Publications. She now lives in Austin, Texas, where she works as a freelance editor and is trying to trick someone into publishing her full-length collection of erasure poems based on women's and teen magazines. She blogs at EKristinAnderson.com and tweets at @ek_anderson.

Birds on a Wire
E. Kristin Anderson

(after Prince)

What would you say if I told you tonight that half a Klonopin
isn't enough? My toes are shaking. My piano is possessed
and my eyes will not stay closed. I open my mouth so you can
see the colors on my tongue. Look at this false start—
ink smeared on the page, dirty fingers curled around nothing.
My guitar is a gaping maw. My printer consumes toner
like a struggling addict. Watch me affix postage stamps
to melodies. Shout into the vapor, curl around telephone lines.
My dad called to make sure I wasn't having an emergency.
I told him I was afraid of falling down and running out of money.
He had to pack a suitcase. It rains and the cracked dirt soaks it up.
It rains and I hear my name in the echo. Jokes make my friends
comfortable and I sink deeper into a pillow, twitch like a shadow
on the wall, yell at the TV. I am afraid to watch you. What I hear
is its own real. That real, with half a Klonopin, is enough.
I email friends. I switch on lights. Curl my whole body into itself
until I am invisible, except not, because there is no such thing.
There is only beauty and emptiness. Watch: I will empty myself.
Give me a tambourine, and I'll dance as it all leaves me—
every birthday, dream, death, try, do, fail. It lands in a puddle
at my feet and sinks into the sand. What is your truth? This is mine—
the one I can't tell my father while he's on vacation. I ate
four cupcakes tonight and now I'm awake, looking for America
in a solid oak headboard, strings falling over me as if I
could remember where they go on those black and white lines.

POETRY

We haven't forgotten about you, motherfucker
E. Kristin Anderson

Show me where it hurts—America will kiss it
better. Show me the purple bruise, the falling
out of/in to the car, the rolled ankle and the shoes
that will never look like shoes again. Show me
thirty years of a reflection you've learned
to accept as your own. Show me where it hurts—
America will kiss it better. Show me his handprint
on your thigh. The vomit your stomach forced
up your esophagus and past your teeth. Show me
the whispers you tried to push out instead.
Show me where it hurts; America will kiss it better.
Show me your sisters—look at these perfect arms.
Did you take pictures? Show me the blood, the scrape,
the clock on your vagina. Show me the clock—
it ticks like an angry child. Show me where it hurts;
America will kiss it better. Hold my hand. Hers, too.
You are a list now. I print it and show them where it hurts.
I watch our daughters. They know where it hurts.
I watch the man. He puts on pajamas. We will not
let him kiss it better. Our sons know the kiss, the clock,
the bruise, the years. Kiss it better, kiss it better.

POETRY

Sometimes Writing's Like That
Jane Attanucci

The bumptious geranium I bought
to brighten the table where I write
dropped all its blossoms at once
or so it seemed to me.
The leaves multiplied and spread
huge, green wide-open hands.

With careful measures of food and water,
occasional pinches and snips , I tended
its flowerless growth all summer.
While in neighboring gardens, I watched
a plenteous parade of lilacs and peonies,
dahlias, day lilies and blue, blue hydrangea.

In late August, as the outdoor cascade of colors faded,
a red, frilly head crowned on my coddled kitchen shrub.

Jane Attanucci spent her first career as a professor of psychology and women's studies. Since retiring, she's studied poetry at the Cambridge Center for Adult Education and the Fine Arts Work Center, Provincetown, MA. Her poems have appeared in a variety of journals, including *the Aurorean, Halfway Down the Stairs, Right Hand Pointing, Still Crazy* and *Third Wednesday*. She received the New England Poetry Club Barbara Bradley Prize in 2014. Her chapbook, *First Mud*, a finalist in the Blast Furnace Contest, 2014, was published by Finishing Line Press, 2015.

Albino
Eliza Callard

She's burning her white tears down her white
face and onto my black arms. She has, today,

heard the word, and just as with any of these
slurs, it's not the word, it's the fear behind it.

The hate. I told Derek that she is the golden
sun-child of our love, but he didn't believe me. Today

my child heard the name explaining her
fatherless six years, and the stares, and the giggles,

and prophesied the rest of her life. She
is a stalk of yellow wheat, and someday soon

I will have to tell her that she can decide to stand out
in a vase of purple velvet tulips or she can pass

among the field of grain. Or will she grow tough from
the winds, part of neither, part of both?

Eliza Callard lives in Philadelphia, in the house where she was born and raised. She likes a good hike and a toasty cup of cocoa at the end of it. She shares her home with a variety of family members, some furrier than others. She has been published in *Stoneboat*, *Hobart*, and *Cleaver Magazine*, and her full list of publications can be found at her website, elizacallard.com.

FICTION

Witch Holes
Mary Crosbie

Johan dragged his cart full of witches up the steep hill, cursing as he went. He had been hoodwinked. The village people had obviously sized him up as a fledgling Witch Hunter, because after the trial, it was supposed to be one guinea per witch, but Johan only received three grubby shillings.

What nettled Johan was that they wouldn't let him burn the witches in the town square. Everyone knew burning witches purified their souls, and Johan procured a box of Witch Killing matches, which had been very costly because the Pope himself had blessed them. But no, the village people claimed to have a wolf problem, so Johan would need to mete justice outside the village where stinking witch corpses would not attract any bloodthirsty scavengers.

So, Johan hauled the cumbersome witches up the hill. When he finally reached a plateau, he dropped his dragging rope and saw that his hands bled from the effort. He spat in the direction of the witches to show them his contempt.

"Foul creatures, and fat too!" sneered Johan, rubbing his hands. He lamented the loss of his last horse, Petunia. He had shot her for food, but her meat was diseased. Yet another hardship Johan had endured.

He took out his pipe and struck one of his Witch Killing matches to light it. All this toil made Johan wonder if the Lord Almighty had him on trial, for what crimes, he did not know. Yes, Johan enjoyed the taste of whiskey. And yes, his temper may have flared having imbibed. Regrettably, he had raised his hand in a blinding rage, and once woke up covered in another's blood, but he could not be held accountable while in such a state. Why would the Lord Almighty create whiskey if He didn't want us to partake?

Johan glared at his wicked charges. It was dead of night, but the light of the full moon revealed their visages. There was the fat one, Goody Baker. She had a sweet, doughy look about her. But they say she lay with the Devil and stole sweets from the church larder. She reminded Johan of a favorite Auntie who made him fudge, so he was relieved he didn't have to burn Goody Baker and smell her chubby flesh sizzle.

The little witch was called Goodwife Schmidt. Her husband cried when Johan tied her up and took her away. She was a pretty thing on one side of her face, truly lovely on that side and almost all good teeth. The other side of her face was disgraceful: a scaly, flaky, livid ruination. They pronounced it evidence of her witchcraft. Johan wondered if perhaps she only required the healing balm his now deceased wife had used for her parched elbows.

The third witch, Hilda Delawest, was blatantly evil, with her bulbous warts, too numerous to count, and her constant cackling. He wanted to gag her with rope to arrest her nasty cackling, but he was afraid of touching even one of her vile warts. He looked forward to executing Hilda Delawest, if not to simply rid the warts from the good earth forever.

He had suggested hanging the witches, but the village people said: "Young man, we don't want the wolves to smell corpses. They will eat all the Christian babies."

So Johan, thinking on the spot, had come up with "Witch Holes," and the village people were intrigued.

"I will bury them standing up so they will never rest," said Johan. The man in the leather vest stroked Johan's arm and said he liked the way he thought.

Johan grabbed his shovel and found a place to dig. He wouldn't drag the witches deep into the forest as he had promised. They would never know where he buried the witches once he covered up the holes.

The witches watched Johan work. Goody kept fainting, nearly toppling the other two witches off the cart. Goodwife would smile whenever Johan looked her way, only showing her almost good teeth. And that cursed Hilda, cackled every time Johan hit a rock or wiped his brow from copious sweat. But Johan kept digging, slinging dirt over his shoulder. His joints creaked, marking his steady pace.

Johan used to be a farmer until his pigs died. He was going to become a preacher, but he didn't have a golden tongue or any snakes. So he chose Witch Hunter. The man who sold him his Witch Hunter license had told him it was easy copper. Johan's back screamed otherwise.

Eventually, Johan had three holes for the witches. He untied Goodwife first, and escorted her to her hole as if she was getting into a carriage. She really had something special. It was a shame about the hideously marked face. It was going to be hard to cover that half-good face with pounds of dirt, sharp rocks, and spit. Johan had dug her hole the best, tearing out sharp roots, giving her ample space for her final rest. She was not a complete monster.

Next, Johan untied Goody. She fell into his arms, sweaty and sad. As he dragged her by her damp armpits, she kept slipping out of his hands. It was nauseating, so Johan rolled Goody like a log into her hole. She landed with a thump and then, she screamed. He had broken her leg. Hilda let out a piercing cackle. He had enough of witches.

He grabbed Hilda roughly and felt her warts under the thick fabric of her dress. He wrestled with her, and he was surprised by her strength. It took all of his might as he pushed her in her Witch Hole.

But something was wrong. Damned Hilda was too tall!

"Oh, Witch Hunter. You didn't dig my hole deep enough. Maybe you're in love with me?"

Then she crouched down and popped back up, lifting her dress to reveal her hideous lady parts.

He raised his shovel to whack her. The shovel caught Hilda on the face. It made a nasty gash, which spurted dark blood. She held her clawed hand to the wound.

"Cruel Witch Hunter. You didn't dig deep enough, and the Lord will make you pay," whispered Hilda from her hole.

"Don't use the name of the Lord, foul Witch. You will choke on your words!"

He could not kill these witches fast enough.

Johan needed to do the speech. He quickly unfurled the parchment.

"You have been tried and convicted of the crime of Witchcraft, and sentenced to Death by Witch Holes. You have lain with the Devil, you're ugly, and one of you had an imp, so I'm sending you all to Hell."

Johan smelled something funny and looked around. Smoke billowed from Hilda's hole.

Hilda held up Johan's box of Witch Killing matches. The witch must have stolen them during their tussle!

Hilda stood straight up and then rose even higher, holding aloft a torch she had fashioned from her dress. She was naked, and it was a ghastly sight.

She swooped down and rubbed herself against Johan, and he could only scream.

Hilda lobbed the torch into Goody's hole. Goody caught fire so fast she might have been a good Christian after all.

Hilda roared through the air, howling at the moon, possessed.

Howls answered Hilda back.

The wolves.

Goody's flesh burned so tastily that even Johan's stomach rumbled.

Hilda took off over the treetops and sailed across the face of the moon.

The wolves' howls drew closer.

Johan needed to get to safety. He tried to climb the nearest tree but could not find purchase with his boots. It was as if the tree rejected him.

Goodwife beckoned him to join her.

Johan crawled into Goodwife's hole. They were so close to one another.

The wolves arrived, excited for the kill. Johan could hear their noses sniffing the ground, tracking the scent of death. He could hear the sound of their teeth tearing away at Goody's corpse, her bones snapping, her now crusty flesh crackling between the jaws of the wolves. Johan prayed they would eat their fill. Goody was certainly an ample offering.

He looked at Goodwife's face, the good side only. She smiled and Johan felt stirrings of excitement. Maybe this is what the Lord had intended for Johan, a second chance for him, no punishment at all. He and Goodwife would survive this calamity, and be drawn close, and he could take her back to his village with a new name. The wolves would accept Goody as a sacrificial offering. The sun would come up soon, and Johan and Goodwife would climb out of this Witch Hole, sanctified.

"Look what I can do," said Goodwife. She removed a sheet of her flesh from the bad side of her face and waved it around like a white flag for the wolves to smell.

A robust wolf, presumably the leader of the pack, snapped Goodwife's waving hand clean off her arm. Goodwife laughed as if it tickled. She then transformed into a dog herself. Not a wolf, but a black Hound of Hell. She set to eating Johan's heart. The rest of the pack descended into the Witch Hole to have a taste of Johan. Red mist filled the air. My, they were ravenous.

Mary Crosbie studied at the University of Toronto. She now lives in Brooklyn, where she murders plants slowly. Visit her website, www.marycrosbie.com.

FICTION

Full Transparency
John Domenichini

The program had a matter-of-fact male voice: "Welcome to the Happy Interactions relationship program. Would you like to start your profile?"

Glen brought the tablet closer to his face. "Um, yes," he said.

"Very good. What's your name?"

"Glen Michael Jefferson."

"Okay, how old are you, Glen?"

Glen paused as his full name appeared in the name field of the profile page. "Do I need to provide my exact age? Can I say 'thirties'?"

"Okay, '30'."

"No, no, no," Glen said, "not 30 exactly." He noticed a slideshow playing in the top right corner of the profile page. He was in every photo, and yet he had never seen some of the photos before. He wondered where they all came from.

"Please respond to the prompt, Glen. How old are you?"

"Well, yeah, I understand the prompt." Glen said. "I'm answering it. What I'm saying is that I'd like to be a little vague when it comes to age."

The outer edges of the Web page started to flash white. "Glen, do you not understand the prompt?"

Glen was mildly distracted by the photo of him currently displayed. He didn't like it. It was too real. And yet, the slideshow seemed to have stopped on it. He begrudgingly returned his attention to the program's question.

"Hold up," Glen said indignantly. "I just said I understand the prompt. You Happy Interactions people advertise how smart and interactive your program is. I'm just trying to ask a simple question about the prompt. I think *you* don't understand."

"I understand just fine," the program said defiantly. "You're being oblique. 'Transparency, transparency, transparency,' that's our motto. I'm pulling up your history in other dating programs now. Okay... cross referencing with Internet search results and a variety of other databases... By the way, we only ask these questions to test the consistency of your answers with other information we're able to collect on you to see how much you're lying."

"What? I'm not lying."

"Well," the program said, "I see immediately that you're 41. You said 'thirties.' Maybe it's just my logic talking here, but 'thirties' seems suspiciously like a lie when the truth is 41. Who knows, maybe you're confused about your age because you're suffering from an early onset of Alzheimer's, in which case we'll definitely need to disclose that in your profile."

"Okay," Glen said, embarrassed. "I didn't realize that you'd be crosschecking my answers."

"Well, now you know," the program said in a more conciliatory tone. "We do this with your dating prospects, too, so you know you're getting honest answers. Honest everything. For example, we choose your profile photo, not you. We want to ensure an honest representation. If you're considering meeting someone new, don't you want to base your decision on an honest representation of them?"

Glen felt a mixture of emotions. He found the program's attitude a bit brusque, but he liked the idea of knowing the truth about potential dates. "Well, let's see if we can get through this profile." Glen said. "You can continue, for now."

"Gender?"

"Male."

"Sexual orientation?"

"What?" Glen asked. "Heterosexual, of course."

"Hmm, it's a perfectly legitimate question for a dating service, Glen. Me thinks you protest too much. Checking, checking... Okay, how about we say 'mostly heterosexual.'"

Glen breathed out heavily. "What 'mostly'? Just heterosexual."

"You know?" The program said. "I must say I agree with you. There's a problem with the word 'mostly.' It's not the right word. How 'bout 'predominantly'? 'Predominantly heterosexual.' That's better. Right?"

"I've got a better idea," Glen said. "How 'bout 'heterosexual.' One hundred percent heterosexual."

"But, what about that time in college?" the program asked.

Glen's face turned red. "I've never told anyone about that. That was just one weekend."

"Good point," the program said. "I agree with you again. 'Predominantly heterosexual' doesn't actually convey your current status, which is what we're going for. Okay, how 'bout we simply say 'Heterosexual, but there was that one time in college'? You see? That keeps it relatively short, and yet clear enough as to its meaning."

Glen stammered. "I don't, I'm not really, I mean, I…"

"Don't you see?" the program said. "This lets potential dates know that you're open-minded, free spirited. If they want to know about 'that one time in college,' and trust me, they will, they can ask you about it. You won't have any of those boring first-date conversations that you get with other dating programs."

Glen didn't want to admit it, but the Happy Interactions relationship program seemed to be making a lot of sense. "You know, it's just… Well, I, I couldn't actually…"

"I understand your skepticism to our full transparency approach," the program said, "but trust me, under the bright lights, you look better than just about anybody. On you, the truth looks fantastic."

Glen could tell that the program's flattery was diluting his cynicism, which worried him some. But from an objective point of view, full transparency in dating did seem like a good idea. "Maybe we can go with your line," he said. "You know, the heterosexual, except for the one time in college thing. I guess."

"Now, you're talking," the program said. "You're going to do fine, just fine. You're going to be very popular with the ladies. You'll see."

Glen felt a kind of freedom he hadn't felt in a long time. Then, an interesting thought popped into his head. "I wonder," he said, "I mean, no problem if you can't... But, I wonder if you can speak in a female voice. You know, to change things up a little."

"Like this?" the program asked in a maternal voice.

"Well, maybe a little younger-sounding."

"How about this?" the program asked in a sultry female voice.

"Yeah, that's good. Use that voice."

"Okay, Glen," the program said with the new voice. "Can we continue with your profile?"

"Sure. Let's continue. Go ahead. Ask me anything. Anything at all."

John Domenichini is a technical writer living in San Jose, California. He has a background in both education and journalism. His writing has appeared in *Foliate Oak Literary Magazine*, *Bartleby Snopes*, and *Mysterical-E*.

FICTION

Rose Salt
Embe Charpentier

On a Monday, crimson roses arrive.

The bruises Wesley left on my arm are as good as a signature.

My brothers rib me. "Marcy, who's your boyfriend?"

"A boyfriend? No way." I heave the roses out the kitchen window, vase and all.

In culinary arts class, tangy basil and tomato tease me. I swipe my finger into my red sauce.

Barry winks at me as he spoons marinara on his crust. "You may be prettier than me, but my food's gonna taste better than yours."

"So cheesy," I tell him. "Not the pizza – you."

His wide lips and red headband stretch tight. Tiny dreads bounce as he tosses the cheese. He glances at my station. "You gonna eat it when you're done cookin'?" he asks. "I got a little brother an' he'd like it."

Our pizzas, gooey cheese sides stuck together, still steam while he packs them in foil.

Mom used to put on her chef's hat for "do-not-miss dinner." Every Sunday, my four brothers and my dad sat down five minutes early just to pound their knives and forks. They hollered, "We want food" until Mom brought biscuits. She basted roast beef in wine, mashed buttered potatoes, candied gingered yams, and iced chocolate cake with fudge. During football season, we tailgated in the driveway.

But heartbeats can go missing. When the two hands that hold you up fall away, you dissolve until the hole at the base of the world spits you back out. Me and the guys – at least we had each other.

Every Sunday for a year, I fried sliders, burned skinny frozen fries, and boiled undrained cans of peas. I sliced Twinkies and dumped pumpkin pie filling over them.

One morning about a year ago, my puffy eyes opened. I turned down whiny country radio so I could hear the wind whistle. I told my dad I had to go back to school.

Now I roast chicken with rosemary, bake sweet potato casserole, and whip up a chess pie without a cookbook. Every Sunday, I bask in aromas and noise.

Dad gives me a kiss on the forehead. "You look good in her hat," he says.

Every Friday and Saturday, Dad lets me drive the Pontiac to the Under 21 Dance. One Saturday, Wesley asks me to go out the back door with him. I won't. He leans against the bar while I dance. I make sure to leave when my friends do, but my car won't start. Wesley and I trade crimson slaps so hard I end up on the ground. He drives off in his father's Caddy. On Monday, it's the rose parade.

One new-moon night, I'm alone with him. My knuckles crash into his jaw. My back bashes the Pontiac's side mirror. I drive away shaking.

Roses again. I move them into my room before anyone sees them. I pull every petal off and leave the thornless stems sticking out of the dry vase.

While I toss the crumble on my fried apple casserole, I ask Barry to the dance.

"Everybody there's white." His voice catches like a broken zipper.

I say, "So what," even though I know it's, "So plenty."

My friends tell me they'll back us up. Dirty looks don't scare poor girls. Seeing Barry on my arm gets Wesley leaving skid marks.

Barry sings when he dances close. I drive him home to a mustard-colored ranch house. He kisses me goodbye like he's pancakes and I'm maple syrup. I don't remember the ride home.

On a spring Sunday, Barry brings purple pansies ripped from his garden. The root dirt rolls into the sink. "Wish we could eat' em," he says. "There's a recipe for 'em in our cookbook."

I run upstairs. Those old rose petals grind up fine in the spice mill. Milled blossoms tint salt pink.

Dad brings home the chicken stock. He stares at Barry for a tick-tocking minute before saying hello. He calls me into the dining room to check the silverware.

"I didn't know Barry was black," he says.

I lean back against the wall with my arms crossed. "Your point?"

"Just that you didn't tell me." He picks up a spoon and wipes it with the napkin. "He's welcome. It'll be nice to have seven at the table."

The Temptations sing our kneading music. Barry rolls dough; I chop celery. He beats eggs; I whip cream. Dad peels potatoes and grills Barry with questions.

"Why you helpin' today, Dad?" My hands tremble a little as I slide a cast-iron pan out of the oven.

"Should've cooked a long time ago. Not like I don't know how." His head and voice dip low.

"Scrambled eggs and grits? Maybe?" I sit Mom's hat crooked on his head.

He taps my cheek with a potholder. "Wisecrackin' on me, Marcy?"

I explode flour all over his nose with a pop of my fingers.

"Lemme get you a towel, Mr. Reed," Barry says.

"You kiss-up." I toss flour on Barry's face. Soon bleached clouds soar. My giggles roll at full boil.

Dad wipes his face with a towel. "You two are cleaning this up." His stern command doesn't surprise me or fool Barry. Dad winks as he leaves the kitchen.

"That eye-battin' was for me, right?" asks Barry. He needs the elbow I shoot him in the ribs.

That night, my brothers pound on the table. My idea? A delicate pansy on each plate. My brother Mark gulps a whole blossom down. Barry pats Mark on the back as he coughs and everybody laughs.

"It's a garnish, you clown." I shouldn't roll my eyes – it's childish. I do it anyway.

"Boyfriends make some girls act all fancy." Mark tries to grumble, but he can't. He's smiling too loud.

After the first table-pounding in a long time, we eat slow and feast deep. The table groans under seven plates of chicken and dumplings, mashed potatoes, and steamed asparagus, sprinkled with rose-pink salt.

Embe Charpentier spends her days teaching English as a Second Language and her nights typing furiously. She's been published numerous times this year in such venues as *Polydras Review, Gambling the Aisle,* and *LitroNY*. Kellan Books is publishing her first novel, *Beloved Dead,* in early 2016.

FICTION

Not Quite Right
Michael Gray

Halfway over the Ashby River Bridge, their burgundy pickup started to slide.

This was on the way to school one Monday. Conner Hamblin had his head propped against the passenger window so he could stare out at the bare trees and white fields, then the ice floes once the river came into view.

When the tires first lost traction, his father swore under his breath. They hadn't been going very fast, but the bridge sloped downhill toward an intersection with Route 17. He dialed the wheel, pumped the brakes. Up ahead, a morning procession of trucks from the Perry Gravel Yard mingled with the commuter crowd.

The pickup's tail end drifted left of center. Conner's dad revved the engine, swore again. As the tires chewed at the black ice for a grip, the boy felt the shift of his own body weight against the passenger door.

Then his father said it: "Love you, Conner."

They hadn't been getting along since the evening before, but now the man looked right at him a moment, all the tension from earlier seeming to channel over to the task at hand.

A shudder passed through the vehicle as the left fender scraped against the guardrail, followed by the headlight. Glass popped, metal flexed and groaned.

But that was the end of it.

Their truck came to rest about twelve yards from the intersection. They were alone on the bridge, the pickup now perpendicular to the double yellow lines.

After venting a deep-chested sigh, his dad climbed out and stood examining the damage. He stooped over at different angles, shaking his head, pulling his coat collar tight. Back in the driver's seat, he said it wasn't that bad.

Still breathing a little fast, the boy thought, but already regaining his reserve.

Conner knew he'd glimpsed something important in his father, a relaxing of sorts in what he probably thought could be his last words to his son. But the moment had passed, the atmosphere constricting back to where it had been.

With one cautious adjustment at a time, his father straightened the pickup and got it back on the road.

"Never do salt these back streets early enough."

The only other thing he said on the matter, almost to himself.

In that small corner of Kentucky there wasn't much physical distance between *city* and *country*, but the social borders were clearly drawn.

Conner and his parents were country. They rented a house less than three miles outside the city limits, a detail that under normal circumstances would've landed Conner in the county school system. For the last four years, though, he'd been attending Prater Independent, a tiny academy that only catered to about three hundred city students per year.

The old red-brick building sat on the summit of a steep rise only two blocks uphill from the nearest county school. Conner's dad worked for the superintendent's office and had appealed for the right to bypass Prater's waitlist for medical reasons.

Conner wasn't a gifted student. At the time of his transfer, the reasoning had been that a change in approach or atmosphere might bring about positive developments. Prater Independent led the region in academics. Their extracurricular activities emphasized chess and debate teams rather than traditional sports, and the students enjoyed a more relaxed approach to instruction. The teachers there had been very patient so far, understanding, but it didn't seem to be making much difference.

Conner was repeating fifth grade this year, just as he'd repeated the third. He was a bit older than his classmates, a bit taller and heavier. In gym that fall a boy, Ronnie Fugate, watched him running laps. Loud enough to hear, he said Conner jiggled like a water balloon with bones. And Conner had laughed along with the rest because he loved to run and maybe didn't understand exactly what Ronnie meant. Always easier to laugh.

Not as fast as the other kids. Not as smart, unless it was math. Teachers would say that in general he was easy company, a good helper, never apt to be bashful or sullen. Just different.

Conner had been called many other things too: thoughtful and cheerful and special and unique. Awkward, maybe. A little off. Harmless.

Not quite right was the most common. His parents never seemed satisfied with it as a diagnosis, but it was enough of an explanation to get by on, and Conner was a boy who needed to be explained. In lowered voices his parents would broach the subject and the newly initiated would soften their guard, sizing the boy up expectantly, but the proof they wanted was in the details and often required even more explanations.

No, he wasn't retarded.

No, he wasn't crazy or even mentally ill, really.

(But the way an idea could get inside that boy's head. Once he tethered himself to a notion there was no derailing him, like when he wore his snow boots all summer long that time, no matter how much his parents scolded or his peers poked fun. If it made sense to Conner, you had to let it play out. There wasn't much else you *could* do).

He'd been born over a month premature, started exhibiting very minor signs of developmental delay around his second birthday. He could read, write, converse, comprehend most things. He clothed and cleaned and fed himself without any more prompting than your average thirteen-year-old boy required.

He just wasn't quite right.

The steep road leading up to Prater Independent was jeweled with salt crystals, though the sun had already done most of the melt work. Conner's dad was able to get up to the entrance without any more problems. He pulled to the curb and unlocked the doors, but neither of them stirred.

Other vehicles came and parked—children hopped down, waved, moved on, but the burgundy pickup stayed fixed.

Something needed to be said.

Conner unbuckled his seatbelt, balanced his schoolbag on his lap. A brown maple leaf tapped down against the mud-speckled windshield.

"You keep your distance today," his dad said. "You hear me?"

Not looking at him this time. Sounding edgy. Spent.

"Stay away from Regan. Don't even say hi, understand?"

Conner leaned over and rested his head on his dad's shoulder. The man gave a slight tremor in response, like he was holding some emotion at bay. "Alright, that's enough. Come on. Get inside."

But the boy didn't answer or move. Not for another thirty seconds or so.

Only recently had Conner's behavior raised any real concerns.

Not even two days ago—a cold, cloudy Saturday afternoon—an impatient knocking at the front door had startled the Hamblin household.

Mr. Turley, a distant neighbor, was greeted and ushered into the foyer by Conner's parents, but the man's errand was not a pleasant one. Before long he was nearly shouting.

The Turley family owned a house two miles up the mountain, at the head of a small neighborhood. Mr. Turley and his wife lived there with an older son from a former marriage.

And Regan, their daughter.

Regan Turley—the lovely name no longer a secret now that it reverberated through the Hamblins' rental house on Old Hallow Road. Conner's parents did their best to appear firm and evenhanded, but barely spoke as Regan's father raged on.

Evidence! Footprints in the snow leading in and out of the woods behind the Turley residence—boots, size nine. The prints were all over the backyard, stamped outside several of the windows, including Regan's bedroom, where Conner had obviously lingered. There was even a wide patch of yellow snow beside the backdoor.

Mr. Turley's voice only grew steadier and more deliberate as the subject of legal action surfaced. "This is *not* harmless," the man finally said. "You keep him away from my home. And my daughter."

With this, he thundered out of the house, leaving the front door open behind him.

Much later in life Conner would come to better understand the concept of euphemism. Not quite right was not wrong. Rather it was the uneasy middle ground that preceded wrong—a state that made others anxious, like watching a scale levering between opposing weights.

Conner had never felt such a tilt in the weights before now. His parents had been astonished at the distance he'd gone on foot, and in that weather! A four mile round trip through the woods to the Turley house. How did he even know where they lived? His mother thought he'd been going down to play in the nearby valley.

Conner hadn't volunteered anything about the other trips he'd taken up to the Turley house, mostly because it'd never felt wrong before.

Regan Turley was new to Prater Independent this year.

Almost twelve, a country girl fresh from the academy's waitlist. Caramel eyes, short brown hair. Her legs far too long for her torso, but so beautiful Conner had a difficult time thinking about anything else when she was around.

Her locker stood across the hall from his. She sat beside him in homeroom and smiled a lot in the mornings when so many others still wanted to sleep. Regan already seemed to know a number of their classmates when she arrived last August, but she tended to be less dismissive of Conner than the rest.

It felt like an invitation, so he'd gotten into the habit of talking to her regularly, though maybe sometimes too often. She listened and reacted so readily that he found it hard to know when to stop, even at those times when she clearly became restless and uncomfortable. Then he would apologize profusely. "It's fine," she'd say, "But I'm gonna go now."

She'd retreat and in a day or two he'd talk to her again.

And so it went.

Seeing her greet her friends that Monday, bright and unguarded, Conner almost forgot about all the trouble with her father on Saturday. In fact, he couldn't wait to tell her all about the truck sliding that morning. It wasn't until Regan took off her coat and sat at a desk on the other side of the room that the thought occurred to him: she knows I was up there—her father told her.

It was the first time Regan hadn't acknowledged him.

Conner felt nauseous with regret. She didn't gesture in his direction and no heads turned to examine him. She didn't point or wince or laugh—nothing at all.

Regan Turley simply ignored him.

One afternoon last November he'd watched, hidden away at the forest's edge, as three girls played outside: Regan with her neighbors Jenna and Molly Combs.

A chilled, sunny, windy day. Bare-limbed trees rackled like bones overhead, but the tall pines running along the side of Regan's house whispered and swayed much more gracefully.

The girls swung from the lowest branches of these trees, all chatters and giggles.

They were trying to muster the courage to see who could climb the highest. None of them made it very far, but Regan froze only a few feet off the ground, paralyzed. Hugging the closest limb, she laughed at her own fear and had a hard time coming down.

Conner was a terrific climber.

His climbing had made his mom nervous so many times, but he was calm and surefooted, always drawn to heights. He almost ran out of hiding to help Regan then, suddenly eager to show her how much better he could do, but the spirit of the girls' game vanished as soon as Regan touched back down to the yard. Not a moment later the three of them darted off to play elsewhere, out of sight.

This memory occupied Conner's mind as the school day carried on, steadily incubating into an idea.

His teachers would say that he *did* seem more distracted than usual. Introspective, maybe. Private.

Nothing that raised any alarms.

Recess for grades four through eight took place in the lot behind the main school building. Many of the older kids collected in nooks along the brick walls to talk. Others played or mingled in the open sunlight, which had warmed the city considerably since morning.

Bordering the far side of the lot was an eight foot chain-link fence, weatherworn and in need of repair. The kids weren't allowed to touch it, but some liked to gaze out through the links at the surrounding mountain range or throw stones over the top.

Just beyond the fence, a narrow earthen ledge marked the beginning of a slope that measured over two hundred feet down to Setser Valley Road. Almost a sheer drop. There weren't many rocks or trees on the slope, but an ashy carpet of winter-dried kudzu strangled the landscape from the fence line all the way down to the road.

Conner knew a secret about that fence, so he waited beside the building's door and said, "Hi, Regan" as soon as she stepped out.

The pretty girl slowed her pace and shook her head. "Hi."

He trailed after her as she made her way toward a group of girls. "My dad told me not to talk to you anymore," she said.

"Oh."

Regan stopped and turned. "What did you do?"

"Huh?"

"Well he was really mad. Said I need to stay away from that Hamblin boy from now on."

Conner paused, not sure at first how to begin. "I wanted to tell you something that happened this morning on the bridge."

Regan looked at the girls standing ten yards away—they hadn't noticed her yet.

"Can I tell you?"

She sighed. "I guess. Hurry up."

Conner motioned her to follow and didn't continue talking until they were standing beside a distant section of the fence.

Once there, he told her about the black ice and the river, the way the truck slid and grated against the guardrail until it came to a stop. He described ice floes and the fractured look on his dad's face when he said he loved him.

Regan seemed decently interested at that point. "You really got in an accident?"

"Well, when my dad said that, I saw something. It just...it makes so much sense."

"What'd you see?"

Conner took her hand and said he could show her.

He pulled at a gap in the metal links, which parted like a small curtain. "I think you're afraid of heights," he said. "You ever been out there before?"

Regan shook her head.

"Come on. It's high but you'll see it yourself. We gotta hurry though."

Before she could plant her feet or protest, Conner tugged her roughly through the gap and onto the ledge.

When her hair caught momentarily on a sharp link, she cried out.

Conner apologized—he was rushing, feeling too eager—but in an instant Regan had turned frantic, screaming, "Mr. Merrill! Mr. Merrill, help! Stop it!"

Shattering his ears. Jerking until he had to tighten his grip.

Students and teachers sprinted over to see what all the commotion was about. Mr. Merrill and Mrs. Lenox yelled Conner's name, but he didn't answer.

They were so near the edge already—if he could just show her. Like the truck sliding toward Route 17 that morning, picking up speed. Even though Conner couldn't explain it, he'd felt the gravity of the moment, the danger, his father's expression—affection superseding everything else. It made so much sense!

Hugging Regan close enough now that he was practically carrying her, Conner tried to explain his idea. But she screamed so loud, and with everyone else shouting in the background—

Setser Valley Road was a narrow brown line over two hundred feet below.

He asked Regan if she felt it yet, but she was glaring at the drop off, wide-eyed, not even seeing him anymore.

"Just look at *me* a second," Conner said, irritated that the idea wasn't working. "I love you, Regan."

He squeezed her a bit harder, trying to force eye contact and aiming to match the tone his father had used.

"I love you."

FICTION

Week in Life of Professor
Drew Guerra

Monday:

They want me to write a love story for them, he complains to Nancy. Another love story, can you imagine?

Love stories aren't your strong suit, Nancy agrees.

Hey now, he says, that's not what this is about.

No, no, baby, your love stories are just beautiful, Nancy agrees.

He goes home to Carole and Rocco. Rocco doesn't understand anything about love stories – Rocco is a dog. He takes solace in this, had Rocco neutered years ago. Rocco will never love or have to write about love. Both are very hard.

He puts on a Schubert recording.

Carole isn't home at eight, dinnertime, so he microwaves yesterday's casserole and writes the love story until he wants to smash his keyboard. Instead, he takes Rocco on a walk. When they return, he tries to get the dog to wrestle, but Rocco is getting old, is worn out by all the attention.

He changes the starlet into a vampire on his third draft. It reads better, is more believable. The leading man stays a man, though. He knows his agent does not like vampire stories, does not want to switch both back later.

Carole gets home at eleven. Her make-up is smudged, she is a little drunk.

Fun night, she says. It is meant to be a question.

Tuesday:

The train breaks down so he misses his freshmen seminar, but that is OK. He hates his freshmen seminar. The topic is "Writing Avant-Garde," and all of his students have nose piercings and tattoos on their wrists.

The grading goes quickly – he has a few good ones, two senior girls in his Hemingway class stand out. He writes "good imagery" for the blonde and "great characterization" for the brunette and he means it. The brunette asks for a recommendation letter.

He spots Nancy at her desk, tries to slip by, but it is too hard. Receptionists see everything.

How's the love story going, she asks.

Good, great, he says. The girl is a piece of work, he says.

Well, you've never written very strong women, Nancy agrees.

He nods, decides the story would be better off without any women at all.

Wednesday:

Molly, the brunette senior in the Hemingway class, stops by to ask about the recommendation letter. She wants to go to Michigan – her uncle says the creative writing program is very good there. Michigan State, if she must.

Interesting, he says. Do you like football then, he asks, those are very good football schools too.

Oh no, she laughs. No, my boyfriend is first chair trombone in the Ann Arbor symphony.

Her hair is almost auburn, he decides, especially in this sort of light.

Thursday:

He wakes up very hungover, with Nancy.

She calls to him while he looks for his wedding ring in the kitchen.

I hear they want the love story by Monday, she says.

See you at work, he says when he finds the ring, hidden in the green vase that Nancy always puts it in, and then he makes himself an extra-large black coffee with four sugars.

One of the freshmen asks him a question about Faulkner's "The Sound and the Fury", which he is not teaching this semester, has not taught ever.

Do you think Benjy is representative of America these days, the freshman asks. This freshman has substituted the nose piercing and wrist tattoo for a

Yankees cap. It is a nice change of pace, but a very bad question. He is not even entirely sure what it means.

Yes, he says. Absolutely.

This has the desired effect – the freshmen ask no more questions all period. He talks about Woolf and Kerouac, Barth and Barthelme. He talks and talks and goes home and talks some more to Rocco, who falls asleep with him in bed.

Friday:

He and Carole go on a date to his favorite Italian restaurant. Every Friday, the restaurant features the same jazz trio. The drummer is very handsome, Nancy observed once.

It's been so long since we've been on a date, Carole says.

Sorry, he says.

You've been so busy, Carole says.

The waiter brings their drinks – vodka martini for her, gin martini for him.

I'd like your olive, Carole says, and takes it.

They sit in silence for a time, let the music wash over them. They have salads, another round of martinis, fish for her and pasta for him. The jazz is very good – he has not heard music like this in a long time.

Eventually he says, You didn't come home last night.

That's true, she says.

The music changes – a familiar tune, he strains to place it, gives up. He would like to forget the rest of the dinner. He signals for another martini, but no one sees. Where has the waiter gone?

And then a man begins to sing – it is "Happy Birthday." A waiter holding a flaming dessert and blue balloons dances down the aisle. The entire restaurant lends their voices to the tune, even Carole, it is contagious, swells into a harmony that ripples across the booths, happy birthday to you, happy birthday to you.

Carole looks across, sees him not singing. She smiles, glows, he has not seen her smile in a very long time. She widens her eyes, urges him – sing! He hesitates, cannot possibly - sing, she beckons, sing!

He falls in love with her mouth all over again, the way her lower lip bobs, thrums with the melody. Carole puts out her hand, red polish on wrinkles, and he is not sure if she means it, but he grabs it all the same, holds her hand as tight as he dares. He smiles back. Sing for me, her smile says.

He opens his mouth. His voice trembles at first, but he pushes, pushes, and the tears cascade down his cheeks where out tumbles a rich baritone. His cry mixes with the others, everyone wishing the boy a happy birthday and lamenting their lost years in a beautiful booming crescendo of life. He sweats his heart out in his hand. He has never been this happy before.

Drew is an undergraduate at Northwestern University, where he studies creative writing, psychology, and Settlers of Catan strategy. His taste in music is impeccable – for playlist additions, he wholehearted recommends Taylor Swift, Ty Dolla $ign, and the entire Hercules soundtrack. Originally from the suburbs of Detroit, he anticipates he will forever be a passionate but dejected Lions fan. Upcoming and recent publications include *Eunoia Review, Flash Fiction Magazine, PROMPT*, and *Helicon Literary Magazine*.

purusha.
Samantha Guss

i can tell when it's going to rain
and what time of day it is

i can intuit things
about astronomy and traffic lights
and how much salt to put in my scrambled eggs

the vedas tell us that we
are all fragments of one spirit
there are three hundred and thirty million gods
but there is only one

and each of us comes from
a divine rib
or elbow
or thumb

sometimes when i stop to listen
i can hear its joints creaking
i reenter the current of my life
sucked in by the undertow
of its cosmic pulse

and knowing this
i can weather the violent jostling
the occasional dislodging
and aimless wandering of my unfastened soul

i am not going anywhere
that three hundred and thirty million gods
have not journeyed before

Samantha Guss is a junior American Studies and Drama double major at Vassar College with an interest in poetry, breakfast food, and taking walks. She often eats a muffin before taking a long walk, during which she thinks about things that she might like to write poems about. She hates citrus fruit. She flosses regularly. She is a Pisces, and a morning person. When she eats animal crackers she takes two of each, to fill her ark. She goes to Whole Foods to steal the free guacamole samples and then immediately leaves. She would like to be a writer or a pirate, but will likely go into marketing or farming instead.

POETRY

the funeral pyre.
Samantha Guss

emptying another container
of rotten strawberries into the trashcan
i think that were i to rescue every rotten strawberry
that my family no longer saw fit to eat
then i would have enough strawberries
to festoon the buttercream crowns
of a thousand birthday cakes,
or enough strawberries to feed one strawberry
to every person who had previously never eaten a strawberry.

enough strawberries to dye the oceans red
for a week.

(still, which is the greater crime:
an ocean full of dead fish,
or a trashcan full of wasted strawberries?)
and i recognize that at this exact moment
i do not have the perspective to provide
a reasonable answer to this question.

so with the ritual discarding
of yet another box
of nearly ten *perfectly good strawberries*
(hapless bedfellows of the one moldy leper),
i say a silent prayer
that these strawberries find a hungry raccoon

somewhere down the line
and that all future strawberries
be saved.

but these strawberries,
the ones that i am throwing out,
are being offered as an oblation
to whatever tolerant god
humors such excesses.

according to the door frame next to the refrigerator
Kate LaDew

the one with the little dents and grooves
from your father's midnight snacks
you were four-feet three inches tall
the coroner told us four-five, the answer to
a sudden question I still don't know why I asked
and I am angry, every time, when I count those two missing lines
thinking these little numbers
these little pencil strokes, the absence of them,
are what will finally make my heart burst
once and for all and forever

FICTION

The Fog
Jillian Grant Lavoie

I wasn't there when my brother, Jack, died. I was 7,000 miles away, in my bed at home in Hamden; or downstairs in my dad's den, watching the Sox; or at work, dropping lobsters into boiling pots at Water's Edge. They didn't tell us the exact time his plane went down.

I *was* there when the green Buick pulled up outside our house. I was sitting on the front steps, smoking, when Cal Chatham and some other guy walked up in navy uniforms, their eyes watching the pavement, hats pressed into their chests.

"Your dad home?" Cal asked, and I wanted to spit in his face, not just because I knew what he was there for but because they hadn't found someone better to come out and tell us. Cal hadn't even made it through basic training before he shot himself in the leg and was sent home to work recruitment. Jack always said he was a stupid son-of-a-bitch. I shook my head.

"I'm sorry, man," Cal said, and he handed me a sealed-up letter. "Jack was a real good guy." Part of me felt like making him get the hell off my property, but part of me wanted him to stay, so I wouldn't have to be the one to tell my dad. It was a couple of days before the Fourth of July, and he'd been all hyped up about riding in the parade with the other parents of soldiers fighting overseas. Now he'd have to go on a different float.

Cal and the other one stood there for a few minutes while I looked down at the envelope in my hand. I didn't want to open it; I didn't want to read the words. I put it next to me on the steps and lit another cigarette, for Jack, and let those guys stand there clutching their hats.

*

Jack got married just before he left for his last tour, when he was living on base in South Carolina. We flew down for the wedding, even though I'm not sure he ever really invited us.

"Kinda strange, meeting his girl like this," my dad whispered to me in the pew. But Jack never did anything the conventional way. He'd shocked the hell out of us when he turned down Notre Dame to join the Air Force. His impulsiveness was catching, though. Three other guys from Hamden joined up after he did. I would've gone myself if I wasn't nearly blind in my right eye.

Even his wife, Meredith, was unexpected. In high school, he'd dated blonds. They were cheerleaders and field hockey players and minister's daughters, and Jack could tell them where to go and what was what. But Meredith was dark-haired and dark-eyed and light-skinned, like a china doll, and she glided down the aisle of the church in a way that almost ghost-like. Jack watched her like he was in some kind of a trance, the way he used to watch his model airplanes launch, far-off and starry-eyed.

Meredith came to us the same week that a thick, white fog rolled in off the sound and settled between the houses that line the Northern Prom. It was all anybody talked about, the fog.

They met in the street outside their homes and on the wharf by the docked lobster boats and in the Kellermans' coffee shop downtown to huddle together and marvel at it. "I can't see but six inches past my own hand," they said. "How long d'you think it'll keep up?" And then, a few days later, when it still hadn't lifted, "What do you suppose the town is going to do?"

It was still something of a novelty by the time Meredith arrived, and so she was able to slip in relatively unnoticed. My dad had put fresh sheets and a couple of new pillows on Jack's old bed, but, other than that, his room was the same as he had left it. I might have taken a few of his pictures and baseball cards over the years since he'd left, but not too many, and Meredith wouldn't have known anyway; she'd never seen the place before.

I watched her edge around the room, touching Jack's things: pennant flags and photographs and posters of bands that had long since broken up. I thought how strange it must be to have been married to someone and not even seen the things that once made up their world.

"I'll let you get settled," I said to her, leaning in to shut the door. She gazed up and straight at me.

"You look just like him," she said, which surprised me, because nobody ever thought that, except me. In the dimly lit bathroom, with my forehead pressed up against the mirror, my eyes turned green, and Jack stared back.

"Take her to the movies or something," my dad said. He was pleading. Meredith had been with us six hours, and they'd already poured through every photo album and box of childhood crap he'd kept piled up in the garage. The three of us were supposed to go out in his old dinghy and spread Jack's ashes in the sound; it was what he'd said he wanted, in case he didn't come back, but the fog was thick as ever, and the coast guard had closed up the marina. Meredith was quiet and easy; she mostly sat on the living room couch, looking at pictures or staring out at the fog, but her presence put us both on edge. We didn't remember how to act with a woman in the house.

The closest theater was one of those artsy ones that shows only documentaries and classic films. If we wanted to see a new release or blockbuster, we'd head over to Westmore or Windham. But Meredith said she wouldn't mind seeing this one independent film about ballroom dancers, so the two of us walked into town and bought tickets.

She asked questions the whole way, like, "Is this where Jack went to school?" and "Did Jack play ball here?" and "How did Jack like this restaurant?" And I gave her answers, "Yeah, he did," "Every season," and "He liked it fine." She ran her hands along the brick wall of the high school and the side of the pizzeria where Jack worked most summers. She sat on the bench where he waited for the bus. She plucked a few blades of grass from the park where he practiced his fastball and slid them into the back pocket of her jeans.

"Can I ask you a question?" I said, when we were sitting in the theater, waiting for the movie to start. It was just us and one old couple who sat far off to the right. "Isn't it sort of pointless to get to know someone *after* they're gone?"

She looked upset for a second, but then she swallowed and smiled. "I *did* know him," she said.

She fished a folded-up picture from the front pocket of her purse and held it out for me to take. Jack's hair was cut short, and he was wearing a blue shirt I'd never seen and leaning against a red pick-up I'd never seen, and he looked to me like someone else's brother.

"It's outside our house on base," she said.

I tried to picture the two of them there, in a brown, stucco, Air Force-issued home, but instead I kept flashing back to this same memory of Jack in high school: standing next to the pizzeria in a white tee shirt, his hair long and shaggy, the way he always kept it during off-season. A couple of girls leaned up against a parked Jeep, talking to him while he smoked his cigarette, flicking at the butt with two fingers, spitting jokes, smiling sideways, making the girls giggle and push their chests out towards him.

I might have been on my way to tell him something or just to hang around the pizzeria while he worked – people did that then – but I stopped a few yards away when I saw him standing there with the girls. He looked like he had a rhythm going. Every nod of his head and turn of his hand seemed to play off the last one, casual but calculated; you could see it in his eyes. And I knew that if I walked up then, there'd be that awkward lapse in conversation. He'd stop to introduce me, and maybe the girls would stick around and ask me questions because I was Jack's brother, or maybe they'd smile and tell him they'd see him later and pile back in the Jeep. And Jack would put his arm around me, and say, "Nice going, buddy," and laugh because, for him, it didn't really matter. There'd be another day and another couple of girls.

I didn't see that Jack in Meredith's picture. In the dimming theater lights, his face looked sunken and shallow and his eyes, brown and hard, like mine.

The fog seemed to get worse at night. It crept outwards from the Northern Prom and blanketed the town in a snow-like mist. Walking home from the theater with Meredith, I looked down and realized that I could barely see my own feet.

When we passed the playground behind Town Hall, Meredith asked if Jack used to play there, and I said, "Sure he did," so she sat in one of the swings and ran her hands up and down the chains from which it hung.

I took the swing next to her and started to pump my legs, picking up the remembered rhythm from when I was a kid. Meredith started pumping too, and pretty soon we were soaring. At the top of our rise, we could see over the fog and straight to the sound, but then the swing would dip back below the surface, covering us in cloud. For a moment, the swings hung just between, and the fog stretched out before us like a horizon. It was almost like flying a plane, like being a speck on the edge of something huge.

When the swings slowed and started their descent, I realized that we were both laughing. Meredith's dark hair was a mess, wild and tossed over her face. "I haven't done that since I was a kid," she said, beaming.

"How old are you?" I asked her.

"Twenty-three."

"Me too," I said, and I wondered why Jack had never told me we were the same age.

Meredith pushed her hair back, and, through the haze, I could see her eyes crinkling and shining in the green glow of the playground lights. "Feels good to laugh, doesn't it?" I nodded, watching her smile to herself. "Your laugh sounds just like his," she said, and I felt my chest sort of fill and expand.

As we walked back along the Northern Prom, somewhere inside the fog bank, she slipped her hand into mine, and the movement was so subtle it felt like second nature. Like we'd been walking that way our whole lives.

On the front steps of the house, Meredith leaned her head up against my left shoulder. The fog hung around us in thick clumps like cotton. I slid my hand along the wooden step so that it rested near her leg; I just wanted to feel its warmth. She didn't flinch, so I moved it closer.

"I'll have to leave soon," she told me. "I have to go back and pack up the house."

"Where will you stay?" I asked her.

"With my parents for a while. Then who knows; maybe California?"

She was staring out into the fog again, and the way her feet kept circling and shuffling on the step, she felt like something wild, like she might take off any second and bolt into the night. I wanted to keep her there next to me. Her body up against mine felt right, like maybe all of this had happened just to get us there that night, like Jack was somewhere pushing the two of us together.

"You know, you could stay *here*," I said, turning towards her. I put my hand on her leg and felt it tense up. "I would take care of you, you know. Not just for Jack." She smiled and went to lay her head back down, but I knew that this was my shot. Like Jack with his girls, if I could keep the rhythm, build the momentum, I could have her for myself. "I wouldn't leave you like he did," I said. I took her chin in my hand, felt her body shake a little in my grasp, and then I leaned close and kissed her.

Her lips were wet and warm, and I waited for them to open and let my tongue in; for her hands, now placed on my chest, to clutch at me and pull me close. Instead, I realized that she was pushing, craning her neck back to twist away. I wrapped my hands around her head tighter, holding her there against me. One more second, I thought. One more second and she'd relax, let me in. She just had to let it happen.

Her breath tasted like warm cinnamon. I pushed my tongue inside her mouth. She made muffled noises and thrashed against me, tried to drive my body away. But it wasn't fair. She'd held my hand. She'd told me I looked just like him. I could feel her pounding against my chest. Any second now, I thought. She couldn't leave. I needed her. Couldn't she see how bad I needed her?

When I pulled back, she gasped for air and sat there for a second, shaking. Her lips were slick with my spit and her dark eyes were kind of clouded over. She got up to go inside, stepping purposely away from me, but I wouldn't have grabbed after her anyway. I'd missed my chance.

I woke the next morning to the sound of the ferry horn blaring. The fog had cleared overnight, and, with it, so had Meredith. On the kitchen table, she'd placed that picture of Jack outside their house at Shaw, only in the light of morning, his eyes didn't look so dark and his cheeks so sunken in. He looked like Jack, and, even with a close-cropped haircut and a strange pick-up, there was no mistaking him for someone like me.

My dad and I waited until the fishing boats had emptied the marina, and then we set his old dinghy in the water. We didn't speak as we steered ourselves out into the sound, past the docks and the last buoy, to the open ocean, the box of my brother's ashes tucked somewhere behind me under the wooden seats.

Jillian Grant Lavoie is a writer, designer, wife, and mother (in no particular order). She holds an MFA in Fiction from Sarah Lawrence College. Her work has been featured in the *Boiler Journal* and is forthcoming in several others, and she is currently at work on a collection of short stories.

FICTION

Perpetual Motion
Jared Levy

My wife Margery has a disorder so unique that it's named after her. Her tongue sticks out of her mouth. Cataracts encase her eyes. Her skin is wet and smooth. She no longer speaks.

The doctor says there is no harm in reading to her, so I do, often. I'm currently reading her *The Tao of Pooh*. Margery loved that book. So did I. Now it feels sufficiently at her level.

Entropy acts according to entropy. Here I am. At night, when Margery is settled, I write, scribbling about life's frustrations creating more frustrations. Some call this a vicious cycle: the circle renewing itself. I see potential.

I take Margery to the dentist. Three more teeth have to go. She grinds them in her sleep. The dentist recommends that she wear a protective apparatus. I'm embarrassed if I could be embarrassed. I silently take the script and limply shake the doctor's hand.

Introduce the love story: I'm in grad school. I feel inferior, as I often do, because I didn't get into an elite program. Instead, I'm at a distressingly small school, all mantras and cutting edge status quo.

I wear a bushy beard. My particular aesthetic is plain colors. Most of the grad students share this dress.

I have an off campus apartment with dusty, wooden floors. I cover the space in antique Oriental rugs. I frame a picture of Raphael's School of Athens. Here, being classical is radical.

I quit marijuana, which was essential to my working habits. Now I smoke a pack a day.

This is all crap. This needs to be plot-driven. This is just listing the events of my life. How about this: before Margery was my wife, I decided to kidnap her. We would drive west and keep going until we hit water. I would bring the few things we needed. We'd travel light. I wouldn't tell anyone, because if it went well, we'd collect her inheritance as ransom and scram to the Mexican border.

I didn't kidnap her: I asked her out on a date. We went to a local Chinese restaurant. She drank three Heinekens and picked up the check. She invited me back to her apartment. She put on Cat Stevens and undressed before I could judge the fullness of her bookshelf. Only after making love did she disclose a few small truths: that she often cried in her sleep; that she brushed with soft bristles; that she loved a visiting professor who said she was brilliant before leaving the school. Three years later, after graduation, we were married.

Alternate love story: whom do I love? The dental hygienist? The pharmacy worker? No. The librarian.

I check out many books, many lying on my nightstand, causing me all manner of pain. But the woman at the library: we trade looks. She's like Margery before the deterioration: bright and sensible. I lust for her, but I'm paralyzed by thought. There're too many obligations, too many forces that control my life.

But goddamn: the librarian. What's new and interesting about that? Nothing. There's little there. It's all crashing down and the pipes explode and flood the library. She's sopping wet and I see the shape of her breasts. She stares fiercely at me. She knows that life is a repeated pattern of chaos followed by meaning making. I have no chance.

The final troubles began so serenely. Lunch laid out on a plaid picnic blanket, supreme bliss: me and Margery on a warm spring day. But at that time it was an achievement to get her out of the house. Her nails dug into the couch, and she looked at me, terrified, silently saying, "Please, no, not this day," the density of her feelings like rock.

I coaxed her out of inertia before we got into a fender bender. The man whose car we hit had no insurance and he didn't want to report the accident. His foot nervously tapped as I explained the importance of notifying the police. Margery, in the passenger seat, sucked the flavor out of a mint, her silent revolt against the day's plans.

There was traffic going to the park. In desperation, Margery stripped naked. The pharmacy was closed on Sunday or else I would have picked up her medication. Instead, there was a bookstore that I visited while Margery raged in the car. A million ways for things to go wrong and only one way where I got a book and she didn't claw up the upholstery.

Waves crashed against the beach. Me, the poor adjunct professor, and her, the wife he married for money, learned to love, and who, years later, began mental degeneration, which, at present, was near complete.

Sitting on the picnic blanket, I looked into her dilated black eyes and thought about how things could have gone differently. I could have been a financial analyst; I could have been a geographer.

Margery stopped making sounds. Her hands violently clasped the blanket and then went limp. I yelled, "Is there a doctor?"

No one answered.

Now I write about perpetual motion: movement sustained without external force. The world acts on me, pushing me forward, and the idea is so potent, I can't let it go. The whole thing is running and I'll never touch it again. It exists in constant motion.

Or I can close my eyes and make this go away. Then there'll be darkness, sound without meaning, stillness to cradle my heart, silent yet begging for life.

I miss Margery. I miss our conversations. I miss my home.

For me, there is no end, only perpetual motion.

Jared Levy was born in Philadelphia, but raised in the suburbs of Philadelphia. After receiving a BA in Philosophy from Bates College, he worked as a paralegal and freelance writer in New York City and then a learn to swim coach in New Zealand. Back stateside, he teaches and writes, occasionally for *Interview* and the Bowery Presents' House List. This is his first published short story.

Error-Prone
Robert Manaster

I'd like to think he yelled down,
But his shoulders twitched
And his chest flinched forward.
He kept a grunt to himself, thinking
I wouldn't notice this urge.

In the lower grandstands, we sat near
A rusted post. My father wore
      His T-shirt and cap.
Only when everyone stood and cheered
         Did I clap and jump,
              Did I yell in a frenzy.
Somehow he tempered excitement
Thinking me too silly of a boy
To stand there awhile. I sat down.
Peanut shells swirled about the sticky aisle.
He held the scorecard, recording plays

In bold-black capitals and slashes
Through base paths. Without exception
He spelled out to me when errors were made.
He complained they should have stopped the rally
 In the fifth: Beckert should have gotten the grounder —
     It was slow enough.

Robert Manaster's poetry and co-translations have appeared in numerous journals including *Rosebud*, *The Virginia Quarterly Review*, *Image*, *The Literary Review*, *Hayden's Ferry Review*, and *Spillway*. His co-translation of Ronny Someck's *The Milk Underground* (White Pine Press, 2015) was awarded the Cliff Becker Book Prize in Translation. He's currently an assistant editor at *Fifth Wednesday Journal*.

FICTION

Torn House
Garrett Rowlan

I've scuttled under the floor for years, specter in the region of dirt. Oh, I've wanted to be a true spook, howling at midnight, freezing hearts and chilling breaths, the way they do in the movies. That's just not me. I'm mobility challenged, as they say, a scuttling bit of consciousness under a house where I once lived.

Nobody's fault but mine: I should not have bought the gun. But we kept hearing sounds in the night, and though they turned out to be nothing more than cats running on the roof, I felt I needed protection. Though I could not protect myself from my own self-destructive tendencies, made worse by alcohol. I suppose I was trying to sear on Joyce's consciousness, as I reasoned in a drunken haze, the importance of her betrayal. You want another man, you want a divorce, well, this is what it will cost you. I put the gun to my head and wasn't satisfied by her shriek. I pulled the trigger. She got a bargain. With a mop and a few crocodile tears she was rid of me.

I flowed into the floorboards, into the absorbent old wood. My soul-bearing blood slipped and dripped into dusty places, leaving a brain without a body, senses without organs, eyes without a face. I now live in a vein of grain.

Yes, Joyce got off cheap, a scream and a scrub, my blood, soaked up by old rags she burned in the fireplace. In the months that followed, she went about erasing my life, no trace, no paper trail, photos burned, and my name never spoken. My son Jack, only a few months old at the time, was told a story about his "real father" who vanished. I became an anti-entity, a nullity, the unheard sound that no falling tree ever made.

Jack grew; Joyce and her lover, then husband, grew apart. Later, I heard the grunt and mutter of some man, his grunting pleasure and retreating footsteps. I heard Joyce's own slow, solitary strolls, footsteps increasingly heavy and shuffling. (I often heard the refrigerator door opening at midnight.) At last, her body hit hardwood: heart attack. Sometimes I think she is still here, a black hole I sense at the other end of the house, one which I have never been able to encounter. Left behind, I listened for her in the boarded-up house, smelled the nutrient-rich earth that has sustained my bodiless binding of perceptions. The homeless men and the partying teenagers have occasionally snuck in, bending back a board around the side of the house, but otherwise it's quiet, the quiet of death that I know. I waited, waited for a way to redeem the error I made.

One day, I heard the hammer fall, plaster shatter and wood break at the house's other end. Cautiously, I oozed to the wall between the front and dining rooms. Above, I saw the light, heard the hammer. It was Genesis in reverse, an illumination at the end of the world I'd known. I grappled up chicken wire and plaster to the point where light exploded into the space from a sledgehammer blow, and I saw the front room I'd known since childhood – fireplace, inglenook, bay window – and in it stood a young man covered in dust. He held something to his ear, and then I realized that it was a cell phone, something I'd heard about but hadn't yet seen. You miss a lot when you're confined to the floorboards.

His speech resonated with familiar tonalities, the grain of my father's speech. "I figure I'd just knock down the wall myself, save having to hire someone. We'll put the tables in the front room and the front counter. My mother's picture will go here."

I saw a picture of Joyce he had set against a wall and I knew what I was seeing, I was seeing my son.

Pride shaped a scar on my limpid soul, and envy too. I was never ambitious the way Jack was, starting a business while in his twenties. That was not like me. I had tried to be a musician, though I had more illusion than talent, a sentiment they could have put on my gravestone, assuming I had one.

In that moment I felt, more strongly than ever, the folly of my suicide. It was in the end an act of spiritual negation and left me only a ghost to my son, his wife, and their unborn child. "Remember you have to eat for two now," he said. He disconnected. He slipped on goggles and a surgeon's mask. He raised and brought down the sledgehammer. Brittle drywall crumpled and dust fell. All things tend downward.

A few minutes later, he stopped in a maelstrom of motes. After he'd rested some time, he looked around the front room floor, filled with dust, grit, and dirt. "A broom," he said, "I need a broom."

He went downstairs into the cellar. I followed. Scuttling through the house, swimming through capillaries of wood, I descended into the basement, saw him standing in a subterranean twilight. Dust stirred in shafts of dying daylight, coming through the open cellar door. He hawked up a bolus of spit. Spat, it struck at the base of one of the wooden pylons just below the kitchen, and flowed down to join the dirt. I scuttled down the pylon and tasted my son's spittle. It was a Eucharist of slime, a spark of spunk. Absorbed, it gave me a new, vaporous sense of mass.

Just then, a box slid from under an old canvas tarp. He noticed. He pulled out the box and opened it. I saw him unwrap and lift a plate made of China into the crepuscular light. I felt my heart leap, for I realized what he had disclosed, a wedding present, exiled in the darkest archives of the basement and free from Joyce's recollection.

"What the hell?" Jack said. He looked in the plate, but the light made it difficult for him to see inside, so he replaced the plate and carried the box and the broom outside and around the house while I fought my way upstairs. Movement had become difficult. I think I know why. My son's spit had impregnated my soul in some corporal way. I had a body, an ectoplasm whose slime made the old system of navigation difficult until I managed to do something I'd never done before, that is, step out of the wall. I stood, a ghost born after years of gestation inside plasterboard and chicken wire. In the front room, Jack examined two figurines, a man and a woman, that had been etched into a plate he had removed from the box.

He noticed an inscription near the rim. As he slipped on his glasses to read the words his cell phone rang. He set the plate on the mantel just above the fireplace. He took the phone and, as he walked into the other room, I moved. On a fog of feet I floated forward. I didn't have a real body and each step was only a comprehensible convention, a mode of motion whose novelty wouldn't overwhelm its purpose. I reached the fireplace. I saw the plate and read the inscription, my ghostly eyes functioning well in this half-light. "Joyce and George Person, November 3, 1985," almost twenty-five years ago to the day.

I pumped a phantom fist. The truth of his paternity would be shown to be a fiction, a twice-told tale whose repetition didn't explain the brusque dismissal of his "real father," who had abandoned the family, I'd heard Joyce say, before Jack was born and was subsequently shot in a barroom brawl. (Leave it to Joyce to make my exit as sordid as possible.) He just might find out who I was. They had Google now.

And that's when I turned and saw Joyce. Death had done her no good. The hair, the cotton-candy fluff so in style at the time, now looked like a hornet's nest, and her angular features were now more skull than skin. Her eyes were all radiuses and no center, like the ring of condensation left by a glass on a table. They regarded me with disgust.

"Why?" I asked her. "Why did you erase me?"

We spoke in ghost, a whispery language, like mist shaped into words.

"He'll never know that his father was a druggie greaser who took the best years of his mother's life and turned them to shit," she said. "You were a loser. You know what was the best moment of my life? Seeing you put the gun to your head and pull the trigger. I about danced on the blood."

She pushed me aside. When I attempted to grab her, she turned and nailed me with a right cross. It had the wallop of a dozen butterfly kisses. Hardly Joe Louis stuff, but when you've been dead for twenty-five years, the legs are the first to go. I fell to the floor. Recumbent, I watched her step forward and press her weight against the goblet, trying to force it off the mantle and send it down to the brick work below, to shatter before Jack could read its inscription. The goblet moved a fraction of an inch as she pressed against it with one leg back and her arms straight as if she were trying to push a car, like that old Ford I never managed to repair. The plate moved a fraction. I struggled to my feet. I lowered my shoulder and rushed. I tackled her, and we tumbled to the ground. She kneed me in the groin just as Jack entered the room.

Together we paused and watched him read the inscription, and when he frowned, his expression told me I'd gotten what I'd wanted, the curiosity and the faint recognition that would lead him toward me. He would ask questions he hadn't asked.

"Don't be a sore loser," I told her.

She kicked me. We tumbled over and over. That's when the floor opened and we fell into earth. Writ in grit we descended, soul to sod, writhing in a parody of the dance that had created Jack, and would send us away from this house and into eternity. Free at last, I thought, free and falling into dirt.

Garrett Rowlan is a retired sub teacher from Los Angeles. He is the author of some sixty published essays and stories, his latest fiction is due to appear in DRYLAND. His website is garrettrowlan.com.

POETRY

Lines
Rebecca Thill

You say, Baby, if I was a painter...
Yet, I know you only sketch in pencil.
Oils and ink are too messy for your careless hands.

Do you think I'm just a lightly drawn line
— lead's grey disguise? Once you said
I'm like a cantaloupe. How I seem hard at first
but soft inside—too soft.

Even though you speak with authority
on melons and canvas,
the bullshit is overwhelming.
Your comparison is ridiculous
and maybe I am, too, for listening,

I'm not your baby
and you're not a painter.

Rebecca Thill recently received her M.F.A. in creative writing and poetry from Emerson College—in fact, so recently that she has yet to buy a frame for her diploma. Since graduating, Rebecca has relocated from Boston to Arizona, but still remains an active reader at *Ploughshares*. She spends her time drinking an extraordinary amount of coffee and trying to write a poem about bears that isn't silly.

Made in the USA
Charleston, SC
03 April 2016